Barrington Moore, Jr.

Barrington Moore, Jr.

A critical appraisal

Dennis Smith
Department of Sociology and Social History
University of Aston in Birmingham, England

M. E. Sharpe, Inc.
Armonk, New York

Published in the United States by M. E. Sharpe, Inc.,
80 Business Park Drive, Armonk, New York 10504.

Published in Great Britain by The Macmillan Press, Ltd.

Library of Congress Cataloging in Publication Data

Smith, Dennis, 1945–
    Barrington Moore, Jr., a critical appraisal.

    Bibliography: p.
    1. Moore, Barrington, 1913–   . 2. Sociology—
United States.   I. Title.
HM22.U6M667   1983   301′.01   82–19197
ISBN 0–87332–241–X
ISBN 0–87332–242–8 (pbk.)

Printed in Hong Kong

Contents

Preface

This study is divided into four parts. In the first part an account of the text of *Social Origins* will be followed by, on the one hand, an analysis of the political and intellectual context in which it appeared and, on the other hand, a survey of reviews. In the second part attention will be paid to the development of Moore's theoretical approach. His essays in *Political Power and Social Theory* and *Reflections on the Causes of Human Misery* will be particularly relevant. In the third part the major political and historical studies will be analysed. *Soviet Politics* and *Social Origins* will be discussed first. Subsequently an examination of *Terror and Progress USSR* and two essays on 'predatory democracy' will be carried out, followed by an analysis of *Injustice*. In the fourth part Moore's approach to historical analysis and political theory will be contrasted with those of a number of his contemporaries. Finally, Moore's work will be related to the concerns of critical theory and the project of 'restructuring' social and political theory espoused by Richard Bernstein. Throughout this present book my objective will be to elicit Moore's approach to the question he regards as central: how may historical knowledge be used by men and women in order to comprehend and master their destiny within the limits of their moral and rational development and the stage of evolution reached by the societies and the global order to which they belong?

Barrington Moore's *Social Origins of Dictatorship and Democracy* first showed me the potential of an approach to the study of societies which is comparative, historical, literate and humane. Returning to that book and also finding my way around the larger corpus of work of which it is a part, I have encountered not only the historian and the sociologist but also the moralist and the political theorist. I have had no difficulty in accepting the verdict on Moore given by Peter Nettl fifteen years ago:

He is a radical of great and austere scholarship who takes nothing for granted and will use the devil himself if he advances understanding. Though he treats those he criticizes with courtesy and respect he is bound to no tradition and accepts *a priori* no disciplinary hierarchy into which he feels he must fit. A loner. (Nettl, 1967, pp.435–6)

I am grateful to Tony Giddens and Jonathan Wiener for their detailed comments on the manuscript. Past and present colleagues have been kind enough to endure trial runs of various parts of the argument, especially Colin Bell and Val Riddell. Once again I have drawn upon the tolerance and good humour of Penelope, Susannah, Edward and Tanya.

July 1982   DENNIS SMITH

Part I

Dictatorship and Democracy

1

Origins and Destinations

Barrington Moore Jr was born at Washington, D.C., in 1913. Having studied Greek and Latin at Williams College he subsequently worked for his doctorate in Sociology at Yale College. During the Second World War he was a political analyst in the Office of Strategic Studies and in the Department of Justice. Moore taught at the University of Chicago before moving to Harvard in 1948. Since 1951 he has been based at the Russian Research Centre in that university. His earliest books, *Soviet Politics* (1950) and *Terror and Progress USSR* (1954), were, as their titles indicate, studies of the development of the Soviet Union. In 1958 a collection of papers on methodological and theoretical issues appeared, entitled *Political Power and Social Theory*. Barrington Moore's ambitious and important book, *Social Origins of Dictatorship and Democracy,* was published in 1966. Moore had been producing books and articles for a quarter of a century before its appearance. However, *Social Origins* quickly acquired a fame far beyond his previous work and guaranteed a ready audience for his subsequent writings, including the splendidly titled *Reflections on the Causes of Human Misery* (1972) and his most recent book, *Injustice* (1978).

A decade and a half after its publication, *Social Origins* deserves recognition as a classic work. It has a rightful place on the bookshelf beside such works as Max Weber's *Protestant Ethic and the Spirit of Capitalism* and Emile Durkheim's *Suicide.* The comparison is not a casual one. All three works bear the bruises of some skilfully directed critical attacks as well as the occasional more brutish hatchet job. However, each represents a major attempt to discover, by rigorous and sustained reasoning about a wide range of societies or historical periods, some of the constants and variables in the human condition. Their themes include, for example, the nature of authority and moral obligation, the functions of misery and frustration, and the expressions of these aspects of human relationships in forms of action and types of social development.

Each of these books attracts attention as a landmark in the literature of the social sciences. In part this is because an element of bravura enters into them all. How audacious to relate the institutionalised pursuit of material profit in modern Western capitalism to the lonely anxiety of ascetic believers before a six-teenth-century god. How bold to employ a science of 'social facts' as a way of explaining a human act so 'evidently' private and individual as suicide. How tendentious to insist that violence and coercion had just as decisive a part to play in shaping relatively decent Western liberal democracies as they had in producing fascist or communist regimes. If the last statement is less provoking than it would have been in the early 1960s then the impact of *Social Origins* is at least to some extent responsible. However, an assessment of this book must partly depend upon a study of its relationship to the larger body of Moore's writings both before and since its publication.

Moore has neglected to ensure that his theoretical and methodological approach is 'institutionalised' and disseminated within the academic world by means of, for example, a large and prestigious graduate school dominated by 'the master'. As a 'loner' Moore has been able to concentrate upon wrestling with the major intellectual problems arising from his personal vision rather than producing formulae which may be readily applied by others. As a consequence the task of critical assessment is both more difficult and more necessary than in the case of, say, Talcott Parsons, a major contemporary of his early career, or Immanuel Wallerstein who has been occupying somewhat similar terrain to Moore in recent years.

The social and intellectual background

When Moore began work on *Social Origins* in the mid-1950s American confidence in 'democracy' and the 'free world' was at its zenith. It was easy to believe that having met the challenges of the Russian Revolution, the Nazi regime and the first decisive grapplings of the Cold War the 'American way of life' was doubly vindicated by two events in 1956. The Suez invasion carried the message that Britain and France had not overcome their old imperialist aspirations. The Hungarian uprising was a great propaganda blow against a manifestly oppressive Soviet regime. By comparison the USA could be presented as a model of virtue. Although there were critics at home and abroad, throughout much of the decade that Moore was working on *Social Origins* the image of America presented by many of its politicians was coloured by a sense of moral and political superiority. In the 'good society' only technical problems remained, it sometimes seemed, and they would yield to manipulation and measurement. Like the physical sciences, the social sciences provided servants of this *pax Americana*. In so far as a professional statement of faith was called for, many social scientists subscribed to the Ptolemaic scheme of things described by Talcott Parsons.

Moore's book appeared just as this world was on the wane. In 1965 nearly four thousand people were arrested and thirty-four killed when the Watts district of Los Angeles erupted in violence. By the end of the following year the widespread occurrence of rioting, much of it fuelled by antagonism between poor blacks and the police, 'made it appear that domestic turmoil had become part of the American scene' (Kerner, 1968, p.38). Meanwhile, in international affairs the focus of attention was being dragged away from Europe and towards South-East Asia. Despite a highly advanced military technology the USA was failing to win a war in a manifestly underdeveloped country. Her opponents were able to exploit not only patriotism and ideological fervour but also the lack of popular enthusiasm for the American presence in Vietnam. Low morale and indiscipline among American troops abroad were already being accompanied by draft–dodging and student protest. The latter became endemic in the late 1960s.

Perhaps the best short description of the American mood in 1966 is repressed anxiety. It was evident that things were not going too smoothly at home or abroad. However, there was a feeling that problems could still be solved through the lavish expenditure that a rich country could afford. The contradiction between simultaneously pouring money into munitions to kill the poor abroad and into welfare schemes to succour the poor at home was not one which many were anxious to explore too deeply. A radical critique of American society had been presented by Herbert Marcuse in 1964 in his *One-Dimensional Man* but his attack was so total and his appeal to the 'far left' so obvious that politically conservative

Americans found it relatively easy to dismiss him. The impact of Moore's book, particularly in intellectual circles, was very different. Here was a man who actually *believed* in the proclaimed values of liberal democracy and did not think that the existence of capitalism was a fundamental obstacle to their achievement. The very Americanness of Barrington Moore made it difficult for radicals or conservatives to ignore him.

Social Origins had been reprinted nine times in the USA by 1975. Moore was awarded the Woodrow Wilson Foundation Award in 1968 and received the MacIver Award the following year. The success of *Social Origins* signalled an important shift of emphasis within the social sciences back towards historical and comparative studies focused upon macrostructural change. A larger and more receptive audience came into being for books such as Eric R. Wolf's *Peasant Wars of the Twentieth Century* (published in 1971), Teodor Shanin's *Peasants and Peasant Societies* (1971) and Roland Mousnier's *Peasant Uprisings* (1971). When Anthony Giddens wrote *The Class Structure of the Advanced Societies* (1973) he incorporated some of Moore's most important insights. Giddens, like Moore, recognised 'the protracted significance of "traditional" land-owning groups within the class structure' of developing capitalist societies and argued that the 'reaction of such groupings, first to commercialism, and subsequently to industrialism, is the key factor which has influenced the form taken by the structuration of the upper class in the different societies' (Giddens, 1973, p.165). This same author was formalising an important part of Moore's argument when he proposed

> as a general principle, which applies to the emergence of capitalist-industrialism in any country, that the mode of rupture with post feudal society creates an institutional complex, within which a series of profound economic changes are accomodated, *that then becomes a persisting system, highly resistant to major modification.* (Giddens, 1973, p.214)[1]

A year after Giddens's book was published Perry Anderson and Immanuel Wallerstein were both in print, each with his own bird's eye view of the movement of human civilisation (Wallerstein, 1974; Anderson, 1974a, 1974b).

When everybody has a telescope and a new map of the heavens there is an understandable tendency to neglect or deprecate the pioneer. To redress the balance, and continue the analogy, we should go back to the late 1950s when C. Wright Mills was playing Regiomontanus to the Ptolemy of Talcott Parsons. It was Regiomontanus (1436–76) who, long before it became fashionable, challenged the assumption that the earth stood at the centre of the universe. The Parsonian world view was similarly challenged by Mills in *The Sociological Imagination* which first appeared in 1959.[2] Mills eloquently criticised Parsonian 'grand theory' and the highly statistical 'abstracted empiricism' of Paul Lazarsfeld. He called for a return to 'the classic tradition of social science':

> Most classic work lies between abstracted empiricism and grand theory. Such work . . . involves an abstraction from what may be observed in everyday milieux, but the direction of its abstraction is towards social and historical structures. It is on the level of historical reality – which is merely to say that it is in terms of specific social and historical structures – that the classic problems of social science have been formulated, and in such terms solutions offered.

> Such work is no less empirical than abstracted empiricism; in fact, often it is more so; often it is closer to the world of everyday meanings and experiences. The point is quite simple: Franz Neumann's account of Nazi social structure is at least as 'empirical' – and 'systematic' – as Samuel Stouffer's account of the morale of army unit 10079; Max Weber's account of the Chinese mandarin or Eugene Staley's study of underdeveloped countries or Barrington Moore's examinations of Soviet Russia are as 'empirical' as Paul Lazarsfeld's studies of opinion in Erie County or in the small town of Elmira. (Mills, 1970, p.139).

It may not be too fanciful to see Mills and Moore as scattered members of an intellectual resistance movement whose members recognised each others' qualities. Moore, for example, had earlier demonstrated his sympathy with the writings of Franz Neumann on theories of power (Moore, 1955, p.107; Neumann, 1950) and on the development of 'the democratic and authoritarian state' (1958, pp.132–3; Neumann, 1957).

In *The Sociological Imagination* Mills described the kind of work which would be in true succession to the 'classics'. It would display the 'sociological imagination' which 'enables its possessor to understand the larger historical scene in terms of its meaning for the inner life and external career of a variety of individuals'. It would 'require a developed carefulness and attention to detail, a habit of being clear, a sceptical perusal of alleged facts, and a tireless curiousity about their possible meanings, their bearing on other facts and notions'. It would demand a sensitive ordering and interpretation of structural variations over time and space. Its problems would be formulated in a way which would include 'explicit attention to a wide range of public issues and of personal troubles' (pp. 11, 141, 145).[3]

Appearing seven years after Mills published his testament *Social Origins* stood up well to examination on the criteria outlined. It represented more, however, than a revived concern with 'specific social and historical structures'. In place of the previous preoccupation with 'value consensus' Moore brought a clear recognition of the centrality of violence, exploitation and the exercise of power in the maintenance and alteration of social hierarchies. Gianfranco Poggi argued that the appearance of Moore's book (along with Gerhard Lenski's *Power and Privilege,* 1966) marked a 'strong comeback of the tough mind' in sociology with '1966 as the *annus mirabilis* of that comeback'. Three notions embodied this 'tough-mindedness':

within larger societies an intrinsically, objectively exploitative relationship typically binds the upper and lower strata; the maintenance of this relationship involves the systematic use of coercion; the critical process is that whereby the productive surplus yielded by the labour of the majority is extracted from it and allocated within the minority. (Poggi, 1968, pp.215–16).

Social Origins: the argument

What follows is not a 'critical assessment' of Moore's book – that task being deferred until Chapter 4 – but an attempt to provide a summary of the main points in the argument as they emerge in the text. Such a summary will help to clear the ground in preparation for a re-appraisal of Moore's achievement.

Moore is concerned with the contribution of the landed upper class and peasantry in major Western and Asian societies to the political institutions which emerged in the course of modernisation. He confines himself to a small number of large and globally significant societies and focuses upon their internal processes rather than the impact of processes outside their boundaries. His object is to produce new historical generalisations and also a check upon existing ones. With respect to his cases Moore argues that there have been 'three main routes from the preindustrial to the modern world' (1969a, p.xii). Bourgeois revolutions leading to 'a democratic version of capitalism' occurred as a consequence of the development of a social group with an independent economic base which attacked inherited obstacles to a democratic political outcome. In carrying out this task the urban bourgeoisie was either aided in its efforts by the rural social classes or the latter's opposition was ineffective. This route was followed by England, France and the USA.

A second and later route was also capitalist but reactionary. The 'political and economic changes required for a modern industrial society' were enacted by elements within a dominant landed aristocracy (p.xiii). Although the urban bourgeoisie remained politically weak, industrial development proceeded rapidly. The political forms accompanying it were, successively, a semi-parliamentary regime dominated by aristocratic reformers, unstable democratic government, and (finally) a fascist regime. This route was followed by Germany and Japan. The third route entailed the effective inhibition of commercial and industrial impulses by the agrarian state bureaucracy. The latter not only kept the industrial bourgeoisie very weak but also left a massive traditional peasantry in being. When the pressures of the modern world finally encroached upon the peasantry members of this class responded by expropriating the agrarian bureaucracy and clearing the path for a communist regime. This third route was followed by Russia and China.

India illustrates a 'fourth general pattern'. None of the three other routes was followed in this case. Although some of 'the historical prerequisites of Western democracy' appeared, the 'impulse towards modernisation' remained weak. The Indian case stands 'somewhat apart from any theoretical scheme that it seems possible to construct for the others' (p.xiii). However, Moore's confidence in the possibility of empirical generalisation is increased by the appearance in particular societies of subordinate

configurations of characteristics which have been dominant elsewhere. Thus it is possible 'that empirically based categories may
transcend particular cases' (p.xiv).

The democratic route

In the case of England Moore is curious to know 'Why did the
process of industrialisation . . . culminate in the establishment of a
relatively free society?' (p.3). Part of his answer is that the development of the wool trade from the late Middle Ages encouraged
the growth of close links between a commercially minded aristocracy and urban businessmen. These links were fostered by a
Tudor policy which sought to impose domestic peace and the
authority of the central state at the expense of feudal habits and
institutions. However, the bourgeois impulse of urban and landed
elites issued in violence against both the crown and the lower
orders on the land. The impact of commercial modernisation
caused English society to break apart 'from the top downwards'.
Groups who were losing out in the long term did 'much of the
violent "dirty work" of destroying the *ancien régime*, thus clearing
the road for a new set of institutions' (p.16). The Civil War was not
a class conflict, in Moore's view. As economic, religious and
constitutional issues crystallised individuals were pulled in conflicting directions. Massive transfers of property between classes
did not occur. What took place was a 'revolutionary' change in law
and social relationships which favoured the rights of property
owners and turned Parliament into a 'committee of landlords'
(p.19). Discussing the enclosure movement, Moore argues that
over several centuries rural capitalists, especially large tenant
farmers, destroyed the protective structures of the traditional
peasant village. Enclosures were a massive implementation of
legally sanctioned 'violence exercised by the upper classes against
the lower' (p.29).

Strengthened through the violence of the seventeenth and eighteenth centuries, the commercialised landed class in parliament
(or, rather, its 'most influential sector') 'acted as a political advance guard for commercial and industrial capitalism' (p.30). Despite a brief reactionary phase, during which the urban and landed
propertied classes closed ranks against the French abroad and

subversion at home, 'the movement towards a freer society com-
menced anew during the nineteenth century' (p.31). The institutional conditions for capitalist growth had already been established and control of the new industrial labour force did not
depend upon state action to any great extent. The aristocracy
retained formal political power and was gradually shifting its economic base from land towards trade, receiving new wealth into its
ranks. Within the context of increasing prosperity 'the landed
interest to some extent engaged in a popularity contest with the
bourgeoisie for mass support' (p.35). By creating a 'popular basis
for conservatism' Disraeli contributed to the search for 'ways to
incorporate the industrial worker into the democratic consensus'.
This period of 'aristocratic rule for triumphant capitalism' was
made possible by the absence of a repressive apparatus, the very
gradualness of the decline of land, and the skills of 'moderate and
intelligent statesmen' (p.29, p.39).

In the case of France Moore's 'central puzzle' is why there was
so much similarity in the 'final political outcome' between France
and England. This similarity was problemmatic, given that 'All the
main structural variations and historical trends in French society of
the *ancien régime* differed sharply from those in England from the
sixteenth through the eighteenth centuries' (p.40). For example,
the French nobility became dependent upon the crown rather than
opposing it. Instead of destroying peasant institutions the landed
upper class drew income from a peasantry which was gradually
consolidating its own hold on property. The impulse to commerce
and manufacturing was much weaker in France than in England.
The short answer to Moore's puzzle is: the Revolution.

In France the upper classes of town and countryside fused not in
opposition to the crown but 'through the crown with very different
political and social consequences' (p.56). Aristocratic commercial
enterprise was centred upon viniculture. Unlike textiles, the wine
trade did not form a basis for industry or for strong links with the
towns. From the sixteenth century onward the crown displaced the
aristocracy as the main administrative power in the provinces. The
nobility was left with 'certain property rights, whose essence were
claims, enforceable through the repressive apparatus of the state,
to a specific share of the economic surplus . . . land was useful to
the nobleman only insofar as the peasants on it produced an

income for him' (p.55).

Through the sale of bureaucratic offices the king bypassed the older nobility, satisfied the bourgeois 'drive toward property' and forged a 'key prop of royal absolutism' (pp.58–9). The costs of this policy included a feudalised bourgeoisie and an inefficient bureaucracy. Colbert, Turgot and others were unable to overcome these disadvantages in their efforts to modernise the economy and strengthen the state's power. In fact, aristocratic initiatives to make exploitation of their estates more efficient in the late eighteenth century caused an increase in peasant hostility towards the political apparatus of domination. Although the *noblesse de robe* and the *noblesse d'épée* concurred in their regard for property rights the bureaucracy was riven with conflicts between members of these two groups. Furthermore, state officials were confronted with bourgeois demands for the elimination of feudal restraints on trade and more radical demands for a controlled and just distribution of wealth free from market pressures.

The conflicts just discussed coalesced with grievances in the lower orders. The peasantry were becoming polarised between rich and poor in response to the pressures of the market. The richer producers were demanding full property rights and repudiating the feudal claims of the nobility. By contrast, the urban *sans-culottes* insisted on price controls, supported the requisitioning of grain and wanted a system of rationing. Unlike the richer peasantry, they were seeking to undermine the market and property rights on behalf of radical notions of social justice. The Revolution eventually came to a halt when the rural and urban interests came into conflict over the question of the food supply for the cities. 'No matter how radical the city was, it could do nothing without the help of the peasants' (p.92). In at least one area the peasantry was particularly hostile. The counter-revolutionary thrust of the Vendée, a district where *de facto* property ownership was widespread and peasant society less polarised than elsewhere, reflected the hostility of cohesive peasant communities to the corrosive effects of the capitalist market. This pattern was later to be writ large in China and Russia.

Assessing the 'social consequences of revolutionary terror' Moore notes the political effectiveness of the violence of the 1790s in restraining speculation in scarce goods and in 'dismantling feudal practices': 'By and large the consequences were rational' (p.102). Furthermore, he argues, the costs of a revolution have to be balanced against the repressive effects of the regime that is being replaced. In the longer term the Revolution closed off the route towards right-wing authoritarianism and fascism. It did this by finally destroying a landed aristocracy which had already been weakened under royal absolutism. The Revolution was carried out 'in the name of private property and equality before the law' even though its principal actors did not include the bourgeoisie (p.105).

The inability of the crown to manoeuvre easily between the aristocracy and the bourgeoisie had made the Revolution difficult to avert. Among the major beneficiaries of this event were the rich peasants who cared little for democracy as such or for 'big property'. Their structural significance in late eighteenth-century French society imposed major limits upon the Revolution, rendering it 'incomplete'. Although not 'inevitable' the Revolution was 'decisive' in removing obstacles to parliamentary democracy. However, its very incompleteness 'meant that it would be a long time before a full-blown capitalist democracy could establish itself in French society' (p.110).

The American Civil War was, in Moore's opinion, 'the last revolutionary offensive' on the part of 'urban or bourgeois capitalist democracy' (p.112). Despite the absence of both a pre-capitalist peasantry and a landed aristocracy Moore puts forward the following proposition: the conflict between North and South might be understood as 'a violent breakthrough against an older social structure, leading to the establishment of political democracy, and on this score comparable to the Puritan and French Revolutions'. The example of the German coalition between Junker land owners and industrialists suggests that compromise, at the expense of freedom, was not impossible within a capitalist framework. Why did it not occur in America?

Moore examines the political alignments before the war between the cotton-growing South, the free farmers of the West and the industrialising North East. Capitalist ideology in the South stressed rural aristocratic and ascriptive values. In direct contradiction, bourgeois ideas of freedom in the North undermined property rights in slaves. During the decades before the war economic and political links between the North and the West were growing stronger at the expense of those between North and

South. The latter were in competition over the issue of whether states newly admitted to the Union should be 'slave' or 'free'. However, there were no economic conflicts with respect to capital, labour or markets which were beyond the sphere of peaceful bargaining. Why, therefore, did antagonism progress to the point of war?

Moore's answer is that although moderate men of property on both sides sought to repress the slavery issue the question of whether the federal state should use its resources to support the North or the South was of deepest concern to politicians competing for power at the centre. Moral arguments shaped in close congruence with economic arrangements were deployed by the manipulators of political power and public opinion. War was made more likely by the absence of a foreign threat, the lack of popular radicalism and the weakness of cohesive links between North and South. Two other important factors were the very contiguity of two societies expressing mutually contradictory political principles within the same polity, and the climate of uncertainty fostered by the entry of new states into the Union.

No frustrated *sans-culottes* or angry peasants were present to exploit a split within the dominant classes which was much cleaner than those which occurred in France or England. Attempts to impose radical reform of the South from above through 'reconstruction' were restrained by those with an interest in preserving existing property rights in both North and South. In fact, sharecropping and informal violence against Southern blacks served to perpetuate to a significant degree – though in different forms – the bondage of the pre-Civil War period. With plantation slavery abolished and new rumblings of urban radicalism being heard in the North the 'classic conservative coalition' between large rural property owners and industrial capitalists subsequently took shape (p.149).

What was 'the meaning of the war', especially its relationship to the development of freedom and advanced capitalism? (p.149). Moore believes that a Southern victory would have imposed a 'dominant antidemocratic aristocracy' in command over a weak and dependent bourgeoisie, an outcome in some ways resembling the contemporary Russian situation. Had there been no war industrial capitalism would probably have thrived but it would not have been 'competitive democratic capitalism' (pp.152, 153). The continuing residual obstacles to the latter derive, in Moore's view, from the incompleteness of the victory in 1865 and the subsequent accommodations achieved between large property owners in North and South. Referring to the early 1960s, Moore comments that in struggling against the remaining barriers to freedom the blacks with their 'active discontents . . . are at present almost the only potential recruiting ground for efforts to change the character of the world's most powerful capitalist democracy' (p.154).

The Asian cases

Turning to China, Moore first examines relations between the imperial bureaucracy, landlords and commercial groups before and after the Manchu dynasty. Subsequently, he discusses the impact of these structures upon peasant society. He wishes to discover not only the origins of communist victory in the structural dynamics of Imperial China but also 'What characteristics of the Chinese landed upper class helped to account for the absence of any strong push towards parliamentary democracy as the Imperial system broke down' (p.163).

Imperial China had no landed aristocracy independent from the state bureaucracy. The extended lineage or clan was a mechanism which linked examination success, the achievement of political office and the acquisition of land for kin groups. The gentry, beneficiaries of this system, made few contributions to agriculture beyond lobbying for irrigation schemes. Share-cropping tenants and hired labourers worked the land. The main task of the bureaucracy was to extract taxes from the peasantry and keep order so that the gentry could enjoy the economic surplus in relative peace. However, it was difficult to maintain the flow of taxes without stimulating peasant revolts. Within these limits bureaucrats made their positions pay by open corruption. This system ensured that the Emperor retained the loyalty of his servants but sacrificed a large measure of central control over them. Furthermore, an oversupply of candidates for the bureaucracy, particularly in the later period, created a reservoir of discontent at the lower levels.

Attempts to strengthen the Imperial bureaucracy after the mid-nineteenth century foundered on the gentry's determined defence of their privileges and the absence of a thriving native bourgeoisie whose energies could be harnessed by the state. Following the Taiping Rebellion the economic base and the legitimacy of the Empire were steadily eroded. Commercial influences increasingly penetrated China from the West. The decay of the Imperial system decreased its capacity to either control or absorb these influences. Although commerce offered alternative routes to wealth and power, under the Imperial system the native bourgeoisie was small and politically dependent. After this system collapsed in 1911 merchants went into alliance with the local gentry, especially in coastal areas. Their object was not to exploit the urban market through commercialised agriculture but to use gangster-like political connections to squeeze a greater share of existing surpluses out of the peasantry. Such arrangements were very unstable.

The Kuomintang was built upon the political base of an alliance among landlords, urban businessmen and military chiefs. Despite its initial populist rhetoric of social reform this movement was directed against the peasantry and a growing urban labour force. Its object was to maintain the status quo. Subsequently, a patriotic and militaristic ideology emerged similar in some ways to Western fascism. However, unlike its German counterpart no attempt was made by the Kuomintang to build up China's industrial base to any great extent.

Turning to the peasantry during and after the Imperial period Moore examines the institution of the clan which, through its ritual and economic functions, provided the main link between the peasant village and the local gentry. Regional in character, the clan was a potential focus for rebellion as well as a means of social control. Within the village economic production was focused upon the household plot. It was governed by market rationality rather than collective solidarity. Atomism within the village and despotism within the family both provided materials for disaffection. However, although rebellions in the nineteenth century undermined the Imperial administration they did not disrupt the local structure of landlordism. Following the Empire's collapse the polarisation of the village due to commercial pressures intensified, producing a mass of marginal peasants. The communists used their growing power in the villages to redistribute land among the poorer peasantry in ways which undermined the influence of the clan and of patriarchal family heads. The frustrations of sexual, generational and class oppression were released for revolutionary purposes. Exploiting not only these forces but also popular hatred of the invading Japanese, the communists forged the means to defeat the Kuomintang and acquire political control of China.

In the case of Japan, argues Moore, there has been neither a bourgeois revolution nor a peasant revolution. The political outcome in that society showed a strong resemblance to European fascism. Moore begins his search for an explanation of this sequence by examining Tokugawa Japan, especially during the early nineteenth century, and the Meiji Restoration of 1868. In many ways the latter completed the work of the former. The Tokugawa polity had imposed a degree of centralised bureaucratic authority upon a feudal system of great fief-holders (*daimyōs*) and their knightly retainers (*samurai*). The latter had lost their military function but retained an ethos of particularistic loyalty to their superiors. Detached from the land, they received stipends. By the mid-nineteenth century commercialisation had undermined this feudal hierarchy, turning the lower *samurai* into a discontented 'lumpenaristocracy' (p.236) while the warrior aristocracy in general entered into a relationship of 'symbiotic antagonism' (p.237) with the rising merchant class. Although prosperous and an object of resentment, the latter class posed neither an ideological nor a political challenge. These processes of commercialisation were least advanced in the areas of Japan which served as a geographical base for the successful rebellion against the Tokugawa Shogunate.

The rebellion, infused with feudal and Confucian symbolism, sought to strengthen the state sufficiently to repel Western incursions while preserving much of the status quo. Dissident elements in the feudal ruling class were able to detach themselves from the prevailing order and put through a revolution from above. In the initial stages the leaders of the rebellion exploited the resentment of a declining *samurai* class but the privileges of that class were subsequently abolished. This act was part of a strategy of dismantling feudal restraints upon capitalist enterprise and bureaucratic domination. A strong residual feudal ethos served to legitimate an authoritarian industrialising state hostile to foreign influences. This route was closed to China which lacked the upper-class militarism, the strong commercial thrust and the potential for innovation built into the relatively loose-knit feudal structure of Tokugawa Japan. Also relevant were certain benign characteristics of Japanese peasant life.

The Japanese village was hierarchical, cohesive and closely bound into the wider system of political authority. As commercial development opened up new markets from the eighteenth century onward, agricultural productivity tended to rise. The authors of the Meiji Restoration could use peasant agriculture as a source of capital accumulation without increasing taxation or restructuring peasant institutions. Peasant revolution was avoided. The main change was the rise of a new class of peasant landlords and the spread of tenancy arrangements less infused with ritual obligations. Central government gave political support to the new class of rentier landowners and simultaneously fed the movement towards large-scale industrial capitalism. An aggressive foreign policy helped to maintain national unity behind the state.

The road to fascism is traced by Moore from the 1880s. Political life was structured by the antagonism between rising industrial interests and gradually declining agricultural interests. There was some lower-class discontent but it was not well organised. Repression of the trade unions was aided by the reactionary patriotism of rural Japan which was well represented in both the legislature and the army. The military bureaucracy, which grew steadily more powerful, resented the influence of big business. However, each of these interests needed the other and the government needed them both. In its combination of domestic repression and external expansion, in its dependence upon the alliance between rural and industrial elites and in its adoption of slogans borrowed from a radical right sensitive to petty bourgeois and peasant opinion, the politics of Japan in the 1930s resembled those of German fascism. In conclusion, surveying the process of Japanese modernisation Moore is struck by the impressive degree of continuity in that society's institutions, especially within the peasant village. The cost of avoiding revolutionary upheaval, he concludes, was fascism.

In India's case, the cost of not having a peasant revolution was a failure to industrialise. Paradoxically, however, this society appeared to have the institutions of parliamentary democracy without having experienced a bourgeois revolution. Nor had there been a conservative revolution from above.

Like the tax-farming Moguls, the British confronted the institution of the caste which organised village life and was 'the basic cell of Indian society' (p.318). Through a combination of economic, political and ritual sanctions and attachments the caste system organised all aspects of social life. Government above the village level was virtually redundant as far as the Indian peasant was concerned. Working against this massive inhibiting force the British stimulated a very limited amount of commercialised agriculture. They created the conditions for the emergence of a parasitic indigenous class of large landowners enjoying the security of the *pax Britannica*. However, the surplus acquired by this class was not, as in Japan, invested in industrial growth. In fact, the British presence created great hostility between the favoured landlords and a native bourgeoisie excluded from political influence. The latter turned for allies against the British to the countryside where a huge rural proletariat was coming into existence. Gandhi organised an effective opposition to the British on this popular base without at the same time mounting a direct attack upon vested rural interests within India itself. His movement glorified the Indian peasant community and Hindu values. The expulsion of the British was accompanied by religious warfare, 'an extreme manifestation of the fragmentation of Indian society that constitutes an obstacle to *all* effective political action' (p.384). Despite the British legacy of parliamentary democracy India still had an inefficient agriculture whose surplus was raked off by a parasitic landlord class. Efforts to change this were not helped by political disunity at the centre. Nor was decentralisation to the regions very effective. As traditional ties eroded in the countryside the political problem of managing the population was tending to become more difficult. There seemed to be no major social interest with a strong incentive to push through a programme of modernisation. The costs of the failure to modernise were steadily increasing. However, modernisation would involve either 'masked . . . or more direct coercion'. Moore concludes: 'As the situation stands, the dilemma is indeed a cruel one' (p.410).

Theoretical implications

In three general chapters Moore deals with 'theoretical implications and projections' arising out of his case studies. His three modernising routes have, he believes, a 'limited determinate relation to each other'. Democratic modernisation made fascist modernisation possible and both in turn affected the character of communist modernisation (p.414). Western democracy has developed through a 'long and certainly incomplete' struggle to check arbitrary rulers and replace arbitrary rules with just and rational ones in whose enactment the population has a share. There are, Moore argues, three crucial variables relevant to the agrarian social structure. The first is the relationship of the landed upper class with the monarchy. If either party becomes dominant this is unfavourable to democracy. In this regard feudalism was a benign influence, enshrining notions of contract, legal immunity and the right of resistance in relations between rulers and subordinates. The second variable is the extent and type of commercial exploitation of agriculture by the landed aristocracy. The peasantry might be detached from the land (as in England), left on the land but subjected to a feudal rent on their produce (as in France) or reduced to serfdom on estates geared to market production (as in eastern Germany). The first form was the most propitious for democracy since it created strong bonds between landed and urban elites and dispensed with the need for political controls over a mass rural labour force. However, democracy could still emerge in the context of other less favourable strategies. For example, rentier arrangements in France contributed to a peasant revolution which removed the aristocracy while the issue of plantation slavery in the USA led to a Civil War. In both cases obstacles to democracy were violently removed as a result.

The third major variable is the relationship between the landed aristocracy and the urban bourgeoisie, 'the chief actor in the drama' (p.422). The development of 'a relatively free society' is encouraged when these two interests fuse in opposition to the crown. It is also favoured when the commercial and industrial class is becoming dominant and the landed aristocracy becoming bourgeois. Three other conditions are that the continued economic security of the aristocracy and its residual antagonism with the bourgeoisie should foster competition between them for popular support, that the bourgeoisie should acquire something of an aristocratic outlook and, not least, that the peasant problem should be taken off the agenda. Referring to outcomes rather than protagonists, 'it makes sense to regard the English Civil War, the French Revolution and the American Civil War as stages in the development of *the* bourgeois-democratic revolution' (p.427). Such a revolution, Moore implies, was possible in a small number of societies at a specific stage in world historical development: before this stage it was 'premature' and afterwards 'anachronistic'. The achievement of liberal freedoms 'in connection with the rise of modern capitalism' has entailed both the taming of the agrarian sector and the disciplining of the industrial working class (p.429).

Revolution from above and fascism are encouraged by rentier agriculture and serfdom. Both have required 'strong political methods to extract the surplus, keep the labour force in place and in general make the system work' (p.434). The Prussian state illustrates the tendency of labour-repressive systems to foster aristocratic dependence upon the state as well as the preservation of a military ethic amongst the nobility. Conservative modernisation is described by Moore in terms of four stages. First, a coalition develops between the aristocracy and the bourgeoisie in which the latter 'exchange the right to rule for the right to make money' (p.437). Second, as the agricultural sector experiences increased competition from technically advanced farmers abroad the impulse towards political repression to maintain the aristocracy's position increases. Third, the conservative coalition of land and industry enacts, often within a semi-parliamentary guise, an economic and political 'revolution from above'. The object is to dismantle just enough of the old order to make large-scale industrialisation possible under the aegis of the state. The threat of foreign enemies and the rewards of increased resources combine to encourage political rationalisation, 'the making of citizens in a new type of society' (p.439). The most successful examples of conservative modernisation had the benefits of able leadership, especially in the landed class, and strong governments which had 'become separate from society' and were able to act vigorously upon it.

The insoluble dilemma faced by such regimes is how to modernise without changing their social structures. Militarism and international conflict repress this dilemma. In the fourth stage, rather than seek 'to use modern technology rationally for human welfare' efforts are made 'to make reaction popular in the form of fascism' (p.442). Following a brief discussion of unsuccessful reactionary trends in England, Russia and India Moore makes the point that fascism is a reaction to a stage of development in which 'the masses' have become politically significant. Through a discussion of Japan, Germany and Italy he illustrates four characteristics of fascism: the absence of a conception of 'objective law'; the rejection of humanitarian ideals such as equality in favour of a rhetoric of blood and death; insistence on hierarchy and obedience as values in their own right to be enjoyed by 'comrades in submission' (p.447); and a plebeian anticapitalism appealing to the lower middle class and the peasantry.

In his discussion of peasants and revolution Moore focuses upon the ties binding the peasantry to the upper classes. A comparison of India and China suggests that a highly segmented society dependent upon diffuse sanctions for its coherence and for the extraction of surplus from the peasantry is more resistant to peasant rebellion than one characterised by a bureaucratic central authority which carries out taxation. Feudal systems fall between the two extremes. In addition, damaging peasant revolts are most likely in cases where the landed upper class attempts to squeeze a larger surplus out of a peasant society which is left structurally intact but damaged by commercial pressures; least likely where strong aristocratic initiatives remould or destroy peasant society in the course of commercialising agricultural production. Moore illustrates this point by a comparison between the subjugation of the peasantry by the Junkers in north-eastern Germany and the resistance of their neighbours to the southwest during the *Bauernkrieg* of 1524–5.

In the course of modernisation rural social classes are subject to two pressures. These are the extension of market relations into the countryside and the creation of strong central government with a far-reaching bureaucratic apparatus. The effect of these pressures partly depends upon the strength and character of the bonds linking the upper class to the peasantry. Typically, in return for a share of the surplus the upper class provides, seeks to provide or at least claims to provide military security, legitimacy for the social order and, in some cases, a judicial system. Where the bonds between lord and peasant are strong peasant uprisings are inhibited. They tend to be strong when peasant and master are not in severe competition for material resources and when the overlord is an active member of the village community providing essential services to which the rewards and privileges he receives are roughly commensurate. In such circumstances the need for force and deception are reduced since 'folk conceptions of justice' are seen to be enacted which have 'a rational and realistic basis' (p.471).

Modernisation tends to upset these relationships. The state takes over the landlord's 'protective' function though leaving him in many cases with his traditional exploitative rights over the peasantry. As the lord's need for cash and his opportunity to sell produce on the urban market increase, the peasantry are exposed to the simultaneous application of traditional demands and new techniques of capitalist exploitation. Revolt is especially likely if the 'upper crust' of the peasantry becomes disaffected. A major point in Moore's argument is that the stimulus for peasant revolt is not merely economic pressure but a feeling that sudden new demands are 'a break with accepted rules and customs' (p.474).

Moore then focuses more directly upon the internal organisation of the peasant community. Although weak solidarity always inhibits political action, strong solidarity may be either rebellious or conservative. In the former case grievances tend to be transmitted through the community, uniting it in hostility to the upper class. Communal sharing of land is the typical basis for this form. The traditional peasant community is a potential source of popular conceptions of justice which contradict those promoted by the state. By contrast, conservative solidarity tends to be based upon a strongly sanctioned division of labour which ties people with potential grievances tightly into the prevailing order. Absolutist bureaucracies are particularly susceptible to peasant revolution. This is because they not only upset traditional landlord–peasant relations but also inhibit the development of strong urban capitalist interests which might give strength to bourgeois democratic tendencies. In conclusion Moore points out that the effectiveness and the political outcomes of peasant uprisings depend partly upon which groups ally with the peasantry. These alliances vary at different stages of economic development but a negative conclusion which emerges is that peasants have seldom been 'the allies of democratic capitalism, an historical formation that in any case is now past its zenith' (p.483).

In an Epilogue Moore develops three themes. The first is that the 'culture' of a group, class or society which 'screens out certain parts of the objective situation and emphasizes other parts', has to be explained in terms of the past and present experiences of human actors in social relationships. Values 'do not descend from heaven' but have to 'be recreated anew in each generation, often with great pain and suffering', through institutions which serve 'concrete interests and privileges' (p.486). Cultural inertia requires as much explanation as cultural change. Both are intimately related to the interests of dominant classes. Second, Moore argues that the reactionary and revolutionary ideologies which accompany modernisation have an important origin in the experience of declining rural classes. One response of landed aristocrats critical of the exactions of advancing royal bureaucracy and the encroaching regime of the specialised technician has been to stress the liberal values of the 'open society'. Ideally this would be presided over by educated amateurs competent to assess the social and political implications of broad issues in all spheres of knowledge. A more reactionary ideological mixture which arises when the rural order is under still greater threat is that of Catonism. By this term Moore means a demand for moral regeneration infused with nostalgic recall of traditional rural values. Such an ideology may be used to justify repressive authority in its attempt to preserve the old landed class. Finally, an important source of revolutionary radicalism is the ethos of equality and sharing which derives from the experience of peasant communities and is transmitted to lesser tradesmen in the towns.

Moore's third theme is that a broad view of the costs and benefits of violent revolution (as opposed to gradualism or inertia) supports neither the position that violence should always be avoided nor the claim that communist revolutions have brought more rewards than penalties to the societies involved. Indeed 'both Western liberalism and communism (especially the Russian version) have begun to display symptoms of historical obsolescence', turning into 'ideologies that justify and conceal numerous forms of repression' at home and abroad. Given the strength of the opposition, 'no commitment to a free society can dispense with some conception of revolutionary coercion' albeit as 'an ultimate necessity, a last resort in political action' (p.508).

The final note 'on statistics and conservative historiography' also makes three points. First, he indicates the conservative bias in three statistical studies (Brunton and Pennington, 1954; Mingay, 1962; Greer, 1935) whose assumptions and conclusions apparently contradict his own view of bourgeois revolutions. He concludes, *inter alia*, that 'it is not only who fights but what the fight is about that matters' (p.518). He suggests that a serious contradiction arises from the methodological necessity of making progressively finer distinctions in statistical data in order to cope with the social differentiation produced by structural change. The finer the distinctions made, 'the smaller and less trustworthy become the statistical piles'. In Moore's opinion, 'At bottom the sizes of the different piles are consequences of structural changes. They are not the changes themselves.' Citing Whitehead (1938), Moore insists that qualitative changes in the way human beings relate to each other (for example as a consequence of changes in the mode of production) are in fact 'incommensurable' (p.520).

Third, Moore asks whether social change can be described and explained 'in an objective fashion?' He believes that in order to do this it is necessary to distinguish between the causes of historical events and their 'consequences or meaning' (p.521). A historian's assessment of the causes of a past event, for example the American Civil War, cannot affect those causes. However, his opinion of its consequences has 'polemical results *now*', whatever his intention.[4] This is because in selecting his facts and ordering them the analyst adopts principles which 'have political and moral consequences'. Moore distinguishes between 'neutrality' and 'objectivity' in social and historical analysis. The existence of the latter may be recognised in the certainty that whatever his moral stand 'any student of human affairs is bound sooner or later to come across evidence that is profoundly disturbing. Then he has the task of coming to terms with it honestly' (p.522). However, since truthful analyses often produce conclusions damaging to the interests of the powerful a stance of 'neutrality' with respect to the status quo would be a retreat from objectivity. On this note the book concludes.

Social Origins: the critical response

The above summary, which deliberately avoids either systematising the argument or evaluating it, is an attempt to 'recover' Moore's text. Over the years a thick overgrowth of criticism has tended to blur its original outlines. Much of this overgrowth, though profuse, is several summers old. More recently the work of Althusser, Poulantzas, Habermas, Anderson, Wallerstein and others has become widely known and much debated. Following the wave of reviews which appeared in the few years after its publication the critical task of evaluating *Social Origins* has slid down the academic agenda. Many of those competent to contribute to this task have been more than fully occupied pouring through the narrow but important breach in the wall of post-war orthodoxy in Western, especially American, social science which was made, in large part, by the success of *Social Origins*.

Turning back to the early reviews an extraordinary diversity of response is found. The overwhelming impression is of a fleet of sea-borne anglers circling around a very large fish whose dimensions are not altogether clear. In the eyes of some it is a Moby Dick to be hunted down and destroyed. To others it is a rare sea beast contemplation of which is a unique source of enlightenment and wonder. Some of the fishing boats have names like *The Good Ship Karl* and *The Merry Max*. Their occupants are divided between wanting to haul in this very large catch and fearing that, large and unwieldy as it is, it might just swamp the boat.

Writing in the mid-1970s Jonathan Wiener rightly considered that the critical response to *Social Origins* 'reveals as much about the present state of social science as it does about the strengths and weaknesses of Moore's work' (Wiener, 1976, p.147). Steven Rosenthal declared that the latter was a challenge to 'the entire trivia and apologia which predominates at American universities' (Rosenthal, 1967, p.30). To some it was 'wild and wonderful' (Harootunian, 1968, p.373), 'remarkable' (Hobsbawm, 1967, p.821), 'a brilliant and significant book' (Gusfield, 1967, p.114). Others were more grudgingly impressed. Reinhard Bendix recognised *Social Origins* as 'a major contribution' and 'an impressive work' but labelled it as an example of 'the Whig interpretation of history' (1967, pp.625, 626). Arthur Stinchcombe thought Moore was 'basically right, but wrong in several detailed, interpretive principles. It is a very good introduction to the politics of modernisation' (1967, p.293).

Gilbert Shapiro was annoyed by its 'variety of digressions, dictated more by the animus of the author than by the logic of his argument'. However, in spite of its lack of 'coherence and cogency' Moore was one of the few people 'playing the game seriously' in the field of producing empirically-grounded generalisations about modernisation (1967, pp.820, 821). David Lowenthal's fascinating critique of Moore's book began by acknowledging that it was a 'massive and impressive book' but fifteen pages later he was fulminating about 'the great harm done to the critical faculties by an imprudent, doctrinaire and even fanatical radicalism' (1968, pp.267, 272). Stanley Rothman was unreservedly hostile. On the first page of an extended review he declared that *Social Origins* was 'marred by a lack of respect for its own sources of information and by contradictions and *non-sequitors* at crucial points in his argument'. Rothman treats Moore as a neo-Marxist economic determinist whose position is 'intellectually and morally untenable' (1970, pp.61,81–2).

Basic disagreements were revealed about Moore and his enterprise. According to one account, for example, he deserved praise for displaying 'as much sympathy for the peasantry as do many modern anthropologists' (Ness 1967, p.820) while according to another 'like most modern urban intellectuals Professor Moore just doesn't *like* peasants' (Dore, 1969, p.303).[5] In Rothman's opinion Moore's approach limited 'his ability to draw moral lessons from history' (1970, p.82) but in Theda Skocpol's view the case studies enabled Moore 'to interpret available secondary materials in a way that makes his explanatory and moral concepts seem plausible' (1973, p.6). Stein Rokkan argued that the 'logical structure' of Moore's argument was 'astoundingly similar' to the model of European party systems developed by S. M. Lipset and himself within a Parsonian framework (Rokkan, 1972, p.137). Lee Benson thought Moore was a Parsonian (1972, p.237). By contrast Harold Mey noted Moore's kinship with C. Wright Mills in vigorously opposing a Parsonian approach (see Wiener, 1976, p.162).

In the course of eighty-three pages Robert Somers converted Moore's book into a multi-factor model whose variables included the following: Groups (including landed aristocracy, peasantry, etc.), Structures (strong central government, bureaucratic administration, etc.), Environmental Factors (external relations, resources), Past Events and Experiences (wars between nobility and crown, peasant uprisings, feudal landholding patterns) and Cultural Values (climate of opinion favourable or unfavourable to human freedom, aristocratic values) (1971, p.367). However, other commentators complained of the *scarcity* of references to factors such as external relations (Almond 1967, p.769; Skocpol, 1973, pp.28–30; Dore, 1969, p.299), the organisation of the state and political decision-making (Almond, 1967, p.769; Skocpol, 1973, pp.22–8; Salamon, 1970, p.101) and the role of ideas and values (Zagorin, 1973, pp.40–1; Lowenthal, 1968, p.259).

Moore was being pushed into and out of other categories besides those already mentioned. Jonathan Wiener reported that 'German reviewers argued that Moore was closer to Max Weber and Otto Hintze in his theoretical orientation than to Marx' (1967, p.162). Stanley Rothman had another point of view. In his opinion Moore's work 'levels a sharp theoretical attack upon models that give more weight to cultural variables, specifically the work of Max Weber' (1970, p.62). An opinion shared by a number of reviewers was that Moore stood in the Marxist tradition because of his treatment of class relationships. Rosenthal described *Social Origins* as an example of 'first-rate scholarship in Marxist writings' (1967, p.31). Skocpol saw it as 'the product of a Marxist scholarly perspective' (1973, p.1). In the eyes of Bendix Moore had produced 'a major landmark in the development of Marxist thought in its period of disillusionment' (1967, p.627). Dore labelled Moore as 'the Bishop of Woolwich of the Marxist school' who, like that celebrated Churchman, was prepared to doubt central tenets of the faith (1969, p.303). Other commentators perceived a less ideologically committed evolutionary model within the work. Shapiro commented, rather tartly: 'any scholar who aspires to the role of Darwin . . . is to be congratulated, if only for his courage. But this work falls far short of filling the bill' (1967, p.820).

Social Origins clearly put the cat amongst the pigeons. Was its author a doctrinaire ideologue or an open-minded scholar? A systematic thinker or a quirky anecdotalist? A Parsonian or an anti-Parsonian? A multi-factor theorist or an economic determinist? A Weberian? A Marxist? A doubting Thomas? One assessment which also draws upon an examination of Moore's work before and after *Social Origins* is contained in subsequent chapters of this book. However, scattered among the early reviews are a few comments which provide valuable pointers towards an eventual conclusion.

Eric Hobsbawm praised Moore's creative practice, so annoying to some colleagues, of 'breaking the taboos of academic specialisation'. As he remarks: 'The author of a comparative analysis does not compete with the specialists; he exploits them and may have to question them' (1967, p.821). This practice is part of a broader strategy which Gabriel Almond has summed up as well as anyone:

Moore's work stands at the other end of the continuum from much of contemporary social and political science. He takes the reader along with him from the formulation of the problem, through the appraisal of the evidence, the construction of generalisations, and their arrangement in an orderly set of propositions about the origins of democracy and totalitarianism in the modern world. He works like an archaeologist, sifting the sand of historiography, picking out the fragmentary bits, marking them carefully, noting the missing pieces, and presenting us with a monumental structure of evidence and inference. He avoids the mannerisms of modern behavioral science, but often his polemics with the statisticians, social theorists, and historians have a mannered quality of their own, unessential and diverting. We are fortunate and enriched by this book, both by its striking successes and failures. (Almond, 1967, p.768)

The style described is the 'grand manner' of the sociological classics.

Part II

Knowledge and Values

2
Certainty and Choice

It is interesting to compare *Social Origins* with an earlier work on a similar topic by a different author which also received mixed reactions. One commentator described this earlier work as 'a labyrinth without a clue, lacking all method'. In his use of sources the author 'almost always mistakes his imagination for his memory'. Another critic, however, thought it 'the best book that ever was written' in its field. Its discussion of topics relating to slavery was 'glorious'. The book being discussed was concerned with the historical origins and sociological characteristics of three major contemporary forms of government. Within it a special place was accorded to the British Constitution and an aristocratic component in British 'decency' and 'moderation' was identified. However, the larger purpose of the book was to find a rational explanation for the apparently chaotic diversity of political forms in terms of a limited number of causes and outcomes. A mixture of inductive and deductive analytical procedures was employed. The author's intention was not only to ascertain and order facts but also to apply criteria of moral evaluation to human behaviour in the political sphere. He was able, for example, to provide a sociological explanation of the emergence of despotic regimes while also condemning the function played by terror within them. In the author's opinion, while structural and historical factors limited the options available to political actors within these limits the moral responsibility for choosing among the options remained in human hands. In all the above respects there are similarities between this earlier work and *Social Origins*.

The critics mentioned above were Voltaire and Horace Walpole. The author concerned is Montesquieu and the book is *The Spirit of the Laws* which became generally available in 1750. In his magisterial study of the Enlightenment Peter Gay describes Montesquieu as 'the first and greatest sociologist' in that era and 'the most influential writer in the eighteenth century' (Gay, 1969, pp.323, 325). The similarities between Montesquieu and Moore are not, I believe, accidental but a consequence of the fact that the work of both men stands in intimate relationship to the preoccupations, prejudices and insights of the Enlightenment. The former was a kind of philosophical godfather to the men of the Scottish Enlightenment in the late eighteenth century and was acknowledged as a profound influence upon the leading revolutionaries in the USA during the early phase of the new Republic. In this new state Benjamin Franklin, Thomas Jefferson, James Madison, John Adams and their fellows believed that they were putting into practice the principles of the Enlightenment.[1] In their own eyes they were accomplishing an unparalleled revolution, creating the first truly modern society free from superstition and oppression, one in which 'humanity, public happiness, protection against arbitrary government, popular sovereignty [and] enlightened policies' would be the 'self-evident' bases for the polity (Gay, 1969, p.566). Writing two centuries after this practical experiment began, Barrington Moore in *Social Origins* and his other writings is providing a kind of progress report or diagnostic assessment with respect to freedom and happiness in America and elsewhere. If Montesquieu was a profoundly influential parent of the Enlightenment, particularly in the Anglo-Saxon and Celtic worlds, Barrington Moore is its troubled heir.[2]

The above statement is, of course, a vast oversimplification. It will not do just to award Moore his periwig and quill pen and label him a latter-day philosophe. It is necessary not only to identify more fully some of the characteristic assumptions, questions and procedures which the Enlightenment brought to the centre of intellectual inquiry but also to suggest some of the ways in which the circumstances of the late twentieth century have imposed a partial revision of this inherited intellectual agenda.[3]

The Enlightenment

Peter Gay describes the experience of the European intellectuals of the Enlightenment as follows:

> The philosophes' experience . . . was a dialectical struggle for autonomy, an attempt to assimilate the two pasts they had inherited – Christian and pagan – to pit them against one

another and thus secure their independence. The Enlightenment may be summed up in two words: criticism and power.
(Gay, 1967, p.xi)

From the classics the philosophes derived legitimacy and a useful
store of intellectual models in their attack upon religious superstition. Their conviction was that in a disenchanted world free from
myths the control exercised by human beings over their destiny
could be greatly increased through the application of reason.

Three aspects of their intellectual approach to the world were
their cultural relativism, their eclecticism and their moral realism.
As information about a large number of societies within and
beyond Europe was increasingly made available in the seventeenth
and eighteenth centuries it became increasingly evident that complex and relatively ordered societies could exist on the basis of
very different religious and political principles from those obtaining in a handful of 'civilised' Western European countries. No
single culture provided the absolute standard by which all human
arrangements must be assessed. There was a similar receptivity to
the diverse schools of thought which were laid before the eyes of
the philosophes as they turned with renewed interest to the
classics. No school was found to be more sympathetic than the
Eclectics who prided themselves on discounting authority and
prejudice in favour of experience and reason as the foundation of
knowledge. As Gay points out, cultural relativism and eclecticism
were closely related and both led naturally to a policy of toleration
(1967, p.163). The moral realism of the philosophes consisted in
their determination to base their thought upon practical experience of the situations encountered by men and women in everyday
life and a commitment to mobilise this thought in an attack upon
the concrete problems of the real world. In confronting these
problems the philosophes wielded two weapons: the rigorous use
of reason, for example in the natural sciences and philosophy, and
an active moral sense. The latter was not relative since the philosophes had an absolute commitment to tolerance, reason, freedom
and humanity as values.

Although the development of professional specialisation
between academic disciplines in the eighteenth century was far less
advanced than it has since become, major innovations occurred
in three spheres relevant to the present discussion: psychology,

sociology and history. Having cast doubt upon the Christian view
of original sin it was important to develop an alternative view of
human nature. There was widespread agreement that human
nature was universal across time and space and increasing recognition that 'the passions' were a natural aspect of humanity. However, disputes arose between those who argued that human beings
were naturally generous and sociable and others who took the
position that people sought their own interests rather than the
interests of others. Meanwhile, in the field of sociology there was a
continuation of Montesquieu's attempt to discover through reason
the conditions under which decent societies came into being. In
Scotland moral philosophers such as David Hume and Adam
Ferguson were turning to social science.

David Hume recognised that there were severe limitations upon
prediction in human affairs but argued that through 'a cautious
observation of human life' and judicious collection and comparison of practical experiments it was possible to establish a useful
science in this sphere (1961, p.7). Gladys Bryson describes the
general approach of the Scottish philosophers as being 'a kind of
rough, common-sense empiricism. They took what they found, but
they did not manipulate or control' (1968, p.17). Such procedures
were employed in attacks upon prevailing myths such as that
concerning the origins of contemporary political arrangements
embodied in the fiction of the social contract. Hume, for example,
preferred to argue that such arrangements owed more to 'The
general interests or necessities of society' (1960, p.229).

Ferguson drew upon both Montesquieu and Hume in his book
An Essay on the History of Civil Society, originally published in
1767.[4] He believed that empirical study of a wide variety of societies would show that despite a multiplicity of occupations, opinions
and desires the underlying character or 'sensibility' of human
beings was everywhere and always the same (1980, p.7). An important aspect of this nature was human inventiveness:

> We speak of art as distinguished from nature; but art itself is
> natural to man. He is in some measure the artificer of his own
> frame as well as his fortune, and is destined, from the first age
> of his being, to invent and contrive. He applies the same talents
> to a variety of purposes, and acts nearly the same part in very
> different scenes. (Ferguson, 1980, p.69)

In Ferguson's view, men and women were active, reasoning creatures with an instinct for self-preservation. The societies into which they were born were a mixture of cooperation and conflict, the latter being an essential part of social life: 'To overawe or intimidate or, when we cannot persuade with reason, to resist with fortitude, are the occasions which give its most invigorating exercise, and its greatest triumphs, to a vigorous mind' (p.24).

In fact, social solidarity within a people depended upon their hostility to outsiders. In this respect, as in others, it was necessary to recognise that a dialectical relationship existed between good and evil, progress and retreat, civilisation and decay in human affairs. A major example of this was the division of labour which increased a society's wealth but at the cost of alienation and inequality. Scholars could not be morally indifferent to such matters: 'Precisely like other social scientists of his time, Ferguson refuses to equate objectivity with neutrality' (Gay, 1969, p.340). The tasks of the social scientist were to identify the social arrangements which lay behind legal and political institutions, to uncover and explain the evils attendant upon these arrangements, and to point out how societies could be improved by human action:

> it may be safely affirmed that the character of man, as he now exists, that the laws of this animal and this intellectual system, on which his happiness now depends, deserve our principal study; and that the general principles relating to this, or any other subject, are useful only so far as they are founded on just observation, and lead to the knowledge of important consequences, or so far as they enable us to act with success, when we would apply either the intellectual or the physical powers of nature, to the great purposes of human life. (Ferguson, 1980, p.3)

Related themes were pursued by Adam Smith and Jeremy Bentham. Although the former emphasised the virtues of a free economy regulated by the 'invisible hand' of competition he recognised the dehumanising aspects of an industrialising society and the tendency of civil government to be a conspiracy of the rich against the poor. Bentham, who had been Smith's disciple, was more sensitive to the evils of the market than to its supposed blessings.[5] He believed that state regulation in strategic spheres such as education and public health was essential (Gay, 1969, pp.366–7, 368).

Accompanying these developments in psychology and the social sciences was a determination to make history into a scientific search for truth. 'Theoretical or Conjectural History' was inaugurated (Bryson, 1968, p.88). This entailed the rational examination of comparative data on social arrangements in the past in order to establish generalisations about human nature and social order. These generalisations would help men and women to make societies better within the known limits of possibility.

Ironically, the pursuit of studies in these related areas also revealed the obstacles to improvement. The philosophes believed in toleration, peace and political arrangements designed to maximise human satisfaction. They opposed oppression and injustice, above all the blight of slavery. Rational inquiry demonstrated the very strength of the forces opposing such outcomes: trading rivalries, human greed and aggression, instability in relations between states, the prevalence of absolutist regimes, and the huge vested interests of ruling classes.

Apart from these practical problems there were difficulties in the realm of theory. In their attacks upon existing political systems and upon the more unreasonable aspects of Christianity the philosophes tended to appeal to natural law, a universal and unchanging body of principles grounded in the nature of man and underlying his sense of justice and fitness. However, their very exploration of the diversity of forms taken by social arrangements tended to undermine this concept of a universal natural law. It began to appear as a species of wishful thinking rather than a scientifically validated generalisation. One popular means of escape from this dilemma consisted in the appeal to utilitarian principles. Based upon the psychological proposition that men and women were self-seeking, Utilitarianism provided a moral test of political arrangements:

> Nature has placed mankind under the governance of two sovereign masters, *pain* and *pleasure*. It is for them alone to point out what we ought to do, as well as to determine what we shall do. On the one hand the standard of right and wrong, on the other hand the chain of causes and effects, are fastened to their throne. (Bentham, 1965, p.1)[6]

The drift towards Utilitarianism which took place from the mid-eighteenth century onwards did not eliminate the fundamental dilemma posed by the need to reconcile the two objectives of freedom and reform. In order to achieve the latter it was necessary to transform social institutions in a radical way. However, the very process of transformation could only be carried out by mounting an attack on ignorance and vested interests through the machinery of the state. Such a programme was bound to place the freedoms cherished by the philosophes under the severest kind of threat.

A revised agenda

In his writings Moore has taken up the challenge of continuing the unfinished work and confronting the unresolved dilemmas bequested by the Enlightenment. The same challenge was taken up by the classic sociologists of the nineteenth century who were, as Moore expresses it in an early paper:

> participants in a single debate about the possibility of putting into practice the principles proclaimed earlier by the French Revolution. To be more precise, they were arguing about the feasibility of creating a rational society under the conditions of industrial advance and with the human materials available at that time. For them "rational" had a definite social content and implied, even if loosely, the kind of society that would enable man to make the most of his creative capacities. (Moore, 1958, p.113)

It is difficult, and perhaps pointless, to attempt to untangle the 'influence' of, say, Marx and Weber upon Moore from the 'influence' of the Enlightenment upon all three. Moore's critical stance with respect to the former writers suggests that in some respects he is nearer than they to the pristine spirit of the eighteenth century. Moore shares with Marx the recognition, which is central to the work of both, that relations of class domination closely linked to economic arrangements lie at the core of society; class struggle is 'the basic stuff of politics' (p.116). With Weber Moore shares the former's dislike of the tendency for conformity and mediocrity to increase within modern societies (p.116; 1972, pp.145–6).

However, Moore is opposed on the one hand to explanations of social development which refer primarily to culture as the major determining factor and on the other hand to explanations which derive institutional arrangements directly from a given economic order such as capitalism. Both styles of theorising, Moore believes, impose too much rigidity upon thought and weaken the sense that social arrangements are the product of human choices. In this latter respect there is an echo of Adam Ferguson's notion of 'man the artificer'. The choices people make, stresses Moore, are made within limits imposed by the stage of social development, the functional necessities of life in society and abiding characteristics of human nature. However, it is profoundly misleading, in Moore's opinion, to deny or diminish the human capacity for choice by using theories which bestow a governing power upon 'Culture', 'Capitalism' or the inevitable tendencies of 'History'.

The nineteenth-century writers are also criticised for anticipating some of the vices which are, according to Moore, distinctive of modern social science. Much of Weber's work is 'an arid desert of definitions. Here begins the tradition of abstract formalism in sociology' (1958, p.122). Turning to *Suicide* Moore comments:

> The positivist tradition begins to produce some odd results as early as Durkheim. Respect for the facts tends to become an inhibition on criticising the facts, though Durkheim's historical perspective saves him from a complete acceptance of whatever exists. (Moore, 1958, p.121)

This historical perspective is shared by Weber and helps Moore towards the conclusion that 'In Durkheim and Weber the virtues still perhaps outweigh the defects' (p.121).

Moore has found himself in confrontation with, or at least asserting his independence from, two encompassing theoretical systems: Parsonian structural-functionalism and Marxism. In some respects they have been the modern equivalent of Christianity and Islam, two world views, likewise associated with competing cultures, which together gave Voltaire such good copy. In their battle against the shibboleths of Christian theology the philosophes of the eighteenth century had a formidable ally. It was Science, the supreme expression of the exercise of reason grounded in experience. Newton's inverse square law of universal gravitation was a sword which could be wielded against Leibniz's defence of God's role within the universe, even if Newton himself refused to wield it.[7] However, at some point between the eighteenth century and the mid-twentieth century the strategic position of Science changed radically. It became yoked to government, the principal source of its patronage. As a consequence, by the 1950s men and women engaged in the natural and social sciences had ceased to regard criticism of the established order as part of their function. That, at least, is how Moore sees it. Unlike his distinguished predecessors Moore has often found that the practitioners of Science or, perhaps more accurately, the ideologists of Science have been his opponents rather than his allies.

In one important respect Moore's link with the Enlightenment is very direct. His first degree was in Greek and Latin and his work is sprinkled with classical allusions. It is, for example, significant that when confronting the central moral issue of contemporary American society, the unjust treatment of the black population, the comparison which immediately comes into his mind is taken from classical Greece. In a passage which perhaps goes to the heart of his beliefs he declares:

> To the critical historian both Pericles and Lincoln become ambiguous figures as he sets what they did alongside what they said and in all likelihood hoped for. The fight for what they expressed is not over and may not end until mankind ceases to inhabit the earth. As one peers ever deeper to resolve the ambiguities of history, the seeker eventually finds them in himself and his fellow men as well as in the supposedly dead facts of history. We are inevitably in the midst of the ebb and flow of these events and play a part, no matter how small and insignificant as individuals, in what the past will come to mean for the future. (Moore, 1969a, pp.154–5)

Although Moore's work taken as a whole displays a striking degree of continuity in theme and purpose there is a noticeable difference in tone and emphasis between the earlier publications culminating in *Social Origins* and his subsequent writings. During the 1950s and early 1960s American global dominance was relatively unchallenged. The Cold War confrontation with Russia in Europe coloured political discussion and American technological superiority in the military sphere was assumed. In his writing Moore helped to dispel a great deal of mythology and ignorance about the Soviet Union. At the same time he engaged in intellectual guerilla attacks upon the complacent view that science was an activity divorced from moral considerations. A recurring theme in his work was the search for constants and variables in the human condition. This enquiry was a major element in *Social Origins* and has continued since. However, in the course of the book's production the political and intellectual atmosphere was changing:

> This book happened to be written during a time when the political climate was conservative and the scholarly atmosphere contained strong revisionist currents against older works that might raise apprehensions about our own society. By the time this book was finished there was already a noticeable reaction against this current. (Moore, 1969a, p.509)

Since the mid-1960s the American establishment has been much more on the defensive both at home and abroad. American capitalism has been subjected to a comprehensive radical critique both for its domestic effects and for its dealings with the Third World. In his more recent work, while continuing to stress the necessary link between morality and science, Moore has also sought to temper radical anger and despair with a careful analysis of structural tendencies in society and politics, the possibility of altering them, and the moral implications of either doing so or not doing so. In other words he has sought not only to bind morality to science but also to harness anger to reason. Moral issues such as injustice have become the organising principle of his later work and exploration of the utilitarian calculus of costs and benefits, a strong subordinate theme in *Social Origins*, has come to the fore.

Science and morality

> Whenever two sociologists are gathered together, to paraphrase a famous remark by Adam Smith, they are likely to engage in conspiratorial complaints about the low state of the discipline. (Moore, 1955, p.107)

In his article published in 1955 entitled 'Sociological theory and contemporary politics' which begins with the sentence just quoted, Moore imagines a dialogue between two such sociologists, one proposing a 'modern' diagnosis of the state of the subject and the other, to whose position Moore's 'own sympathies incline rather strongly', proposing an 'old-fashioned' view. Crudely, the latter view is that many important aspects of societies do 'not display the regularly recurring uniformities that are the necessary empirical basis of scientific generalisation'. Instead 'we have to take nature as it comes . . . and cannot impose arbitrary uniformities where none exist'. Attempts to construct 'a grand analytical scheme' are no more than 'the mere ordering of words or symbols into categories'. The 'old-fashioned' sociologist has a greater task: to solve problems and discover concrete relationships, to investigate 'the retreat and transformation of the capitalist order, the rise of totalitarianism, or the colonial revolution' (pp.107, 108, 109). The diagnosis is developed further in 'Strategy in social science', a paper contained in *Political Power and Social Theory* which appeared three years later:

> When we set the dominant body of current thinking against important figures in the nineteenth century, the following differences emerge. First of all, the critical spirit has all but disappeared. Second, modern sociology, and perhaps to a lesser degree also modern political science, economic, and psychology, are a historical. Third, modern social science tends to be abstract and formal. In research, social science today displays considerable technical virtuosity. But this virtuosity is at the expense of content. Modern sociology has less to say about society than it did fifty years ago. (Moore, 1958, p.123)

Moore's views on the state of the social sciences in the 1950s make pertinent reading in the 1980s for two reasons. First, abstract and formal theorising is still common currency – although in Europe at least its practitioners tend to think of themselves as radical rather than conservative, and quote Poulantzas, Althusser or Castells rather than Parsons. Second, Moore offers a prescription for critical social science which is an alternative to the 'critical theory' exemplified, in their different ways, by Herbert Marcuse and Jürgen Habermas. This latter theme will be developed in later chapters.

Before turning to Moore's own 'strategy'[8] his analysis of the condition of social science under the American '*ancien régime*' will be considered.[9] In a paper which originally appeared in 1953 entitled 'The new scholasticism and the study of politics' Moore distinguishes four tendencies in the approaches to political analysis which might be taken by social scientists, depending on their view of the logic of scientific analysis and their ethical position with respect to their subject matter.[10] Practitioners might define their task as being the collection of facts (empiricism) or the elaboration of abstract categories and the specification of their relationship (deductive formalism). At the same time they might incline towards 'a thoroughgoing relativism and ethical neutrality' (ethical relativism) or take the opposite position (moral absolutism). Having distinguished these positions (p.89), Moore discusses their strengths and weaknesses. The following account of his opinions draws upon all three of the articles mentioned above.

Some of Moore's criticisms of the empiricist and ethical relativist positions, which he treats as being closely related, are familiar. They resemble in some respects those made by C. Wright Mills whose *Sociological Imagination* was published shortly after Moore's own views appeared. Moore argues that an undue preoccupation with the collection, classification and measurement of facts in order to produce quantifiable results is the result of a delusion. This delusion is that measurement bestows certainty and significance upon the 'facts' collected. Instead it is liable to result in 'the piling up of disconnected trivialities' (1958, p.93). The positivist's preoccupation with technique can extend our powers of observation, help to check logical errors and indicate new areas of investigation. However, 'technique alone cannot define what is worth investigating'.

In fact 'Larger problems of the social milieu and, ultimately, of philosophy enter into any defensible judgement of scientific problems' (pp.93–4). The uniformities in behaviour which Moore believes *are* worth investigating concern 'important problems, such as freedom and compulsion'. Such problems are not defined in terms of whatever happens to be easily measurable. Judgements about what is 'important' or 'significant' should instead flow from an understanding of the long-term development of central aspects of human societies such as 'the major historical forms of domination'. However, it is not sufficient to treat history as 'merely a

storehouse of examples' from the analysis of which 'one can supposedly discover the social correlates of democracy, tyranny, class
struggle, class peace, and the like' (pp.130–1).

Moore is speaking from sorry experience. With commendable
candour he refers in a footnote to early work of his own which
'displays all the faults criticised here' (p.208). In his doctoral thesis
at Yale, entitled 'Social stratification: a study in cultural sociology'
Moore attempts, *inter alia*, to obtain 'a rough quantitative check'
on two hypotheses: that 'the presence or absence of social stratification in any society is related to the number and importance of
control hierarchies in the society'; and that 'in stratified societies
the key control positions will be concentrated in the upper strata,
and the positions of no control and authority in the lower strata,
with the minor control positions falling somewhere in between'
(1942, p.230). The above quotation is taken from a paper based on
this work which appeared in *Sociometry* in August 1942 when
Moore was based at the Department of Justice in Washington,
DC. In carrying out this investigation Moore tests his hypotheses
'on a cross cultural basis against the facts of thirty-six societies'
including the Azande, the Aztecs and 'Yankee City' (p.240). This
paper contains several statistical calculations and, perhaps not
surprisingly, tends to confirm the original hypotheses. The influence of G. P. Murdoch, director of the Cross Cultural Study, is
evident and duly acknowledged (pp.230, 250).

Three years later a further article appeared, this time in *American Sociological Review*, based upon the same research data. It is
clear from reading it that Moore is already struggling against the
limitations of the static view of societies imposed by the above
framework. It is entitled 'A comparative analysis of the class
struggle' and seeks to discover whether 'the stability of the economic structure of a particular society' is related in any way to 'the
presence or absence of a class struggle in that society' (1945, p.32).
Change over time is considered, indirectly at least, since stability is
effectively defined as the absence of change 'for a generation or
more' (p.32). Moore is already working towards a new position,
albeit sketchily. He insists that his 'objective is not so much the
statement of sociological laws as to discover possible combinations
of situations and their results'. Furthermore, 'it is often possible to
learn as much from the exceptions to a generalisation as from the
generalisation itself', for example with respect to India. He antici-

pates a theme later to preoccupy him in *Social Origins* by re-marking that Indian experience 'illustrates clearly the point that misery does not necessarily bring about a class struggle' (pp.33, 34). A further question already in his mind concerns the possible class struggles which are likely to develop 'if the entire Orient evolves from colonial status and competes with Western Europe and the USA due to the increased spread of industrial techniques' (p.35). Apart from these interesting anticipations the above work provides evidence that Moore's strictures against the pursuit of scientific laws through statistical techniques are the product of hard-won experience.[11]

A second tendency in the social sciences criticised by Moore in the 1950s is the attempt by deductive formalists such as Talcott Parsons to generate universal propositions which are, in effect 'a collection of verbal categories, empty file drawers, as it were, that are arranged in a neat and, at first glance, imposing pattern' (1958, p.98). Whereas the generalisations of empiricists tend to be nar-row and trivial, those made by formalist 'neo-scholastics' are either so vague as to mean almost anything, or made without reference to the observed world apart from the use of 'illustrative' facts (pp.98–100).

However, Moore is cautiously sympathetic to the attempts made by, for example, Marion Levy to identify a limited number of 'functional imperatives' or necessary tasks which have to be per-formed for societies to continue (pp. 100–1; 1955, pp.111–12). He accepts that functionalist theories provide limited explanations of certain kinds of change in terms of an inherent tendency for institutions within a society to move towards 'equilibrium'. In order to perform functional imperatives effectively institutions have to be compatible with each other. Moore further recognises that 'process' theories such as those of Marx and Durkheim also incorporate 'some view of the inherent compatability or incompa-tibility of two or more social institutions'. As he points out, 'the very notion of predictable change is impossible without some idea of the orderly relation between the parts in whatever is changing' (1955, pp.111, 112). Nevertheless, Moore believes that Levy 'underemphasizes the partial autonomy of various fields of human behaviour' (1958, p.103). Many of these points are, of course, much more familiar now than they were a quarter of a century ago.

In his discussion of the position which he labels 'moral absolutism' Moore's own stance as a student of society begins to appear more clearly. Confidently setting aside prevailing philosophical tendencies he raises the hope that it might indeed be possible 'to construct a system of values or to find a rational basis for criticising and evaluating society and moral behaviour' (p.106). With this sentence, which first appeared in 1953, Moore declares his determination to reoccupy territory which had been securely held in the eighteenth century but from which social scientists had been steadily retreating ever since. Twenty-five years later Moore is still engaged in the same mission. The first chapter of *Injustice* begins as follows:

> Once upon a time in those happy days when students of human affairs were sure of their ground, it was possible to draw a sharp distinction between a political and social system based upon force and fraud and one based upon rational authority and justice. Even if it might be rather difficult to find a convincing empirical example of a just society, this distinction appeared to be an elementary and obvious one. By the end of the nineteenth century this pleasant certainty had largely crumbled away under the onslaught of ideas that by now have become part of the intellectual fare conveyed in fifty-minute portions at many of our universities . . . To recapture old certainties is . . . out of the question, at least in the form they once existed. Nevertheless, there are grounds for suspecting that the welter of moral codes may conceal a certain unity of original form, as well as a discernible drift in a single direction, and that variations from this pattern of a single basic form undergoing prolonged historical modification are explicable in general terms. It is at least just barely possible that human affairs do make sense after all. (Moore, 1978, pp.3–4)

Moore's position as expressed in the 1950s under the influence of the writings of Morris Cohen (1953) and George Santayana (1948) is that if science is defined as 'disciplined and rational thinking' then it can be asserted that 'Science starts from observations but, by a process of reflection, open to verification at every step, it gradually reaches objective criteria for judging the facts' (1958, p.107). In this way the rational framework underlying the external world may be discovered. The perfect circle, for example, may not exist in nature but the idea of the perfect circle may be arrived at by man through a process of abstraction and definition. 'From very rough approximations in nature, such as the end of a log, he gradually works his way to the ideal concept' which provides a means of understanding and evaluating phenomena such as wheels which are not perfect circles but which may approach that ideal. Moore hopes that 'the concept of a perfect society' might be reached in the same way, 'taking off from real societies, to reach a critical standard' (p.108). He adds, in words which anticipate *Injustice*: 'Perhaps the best we can do at any given moment in history is to draw out the potentialities of the social forms that exist before us in such a way as to set up a critical standard for evaluating the status quo' (p.108).

Explicitly rejecting the Kantian objection that concepts are prior to facts Moore asserts that knowledge of concepts is achieved by the manipulation of data and reflection upon it. 'Finding the logical structure of the universe is an act of discovery' (p.109). In fact, Moore argues that his own position in values is 'basically the conclusion that Hegel offers us at the end of his contradictions, when they are stripped of their mystical and quasi-mystical overtones' (p.108). A very brief detour to identify some aspects of Hegel's position may help to explain its appeal to Moore. Hegel believes that one of the philosopher's tasks is to articulate clearly the concepts expressed through the thoughts and behaviour of ordinary people in societies. Ways of thinking and behaving differ between historical epochs and between types of society. However, there is a recurring relationship among freedom, reason and morality. In any particular epoch freedom is defined through rational analysis of the obstacles which existing social forms present to the realisation of the goals and values possessed by members of that society. The limits upon man's potential for freedom in any epoch are determined by the level of reason achieved since the latter is a precondition for the assumption of moral responsibility without which freedom is meaningless. The criteria of morality derive from the society in which the individual exists and express a normative order enshrining values and goals which are indispensable to that society's continued existence. However, Hegel believes that there is a tendency for the progressive articulation of such values and goals in a society to heighten the consciousness of the society's members that the institutions of the society, which generate those very ways of thinking, are preventing the valued objectives from being fully realised. As a consequence the society is liable to be radically transformed, being succeeded by a new kind of society in which new ideas can develop.

Moore's approach seems to have been deeply influenced by the suggestion that the moral order appropriate to any particular society has a necessary connection with the institutional forms within which thought and practice are expressed, for example, the division of labour and forms of domination. He also assumes that the appropriate morality, though implicit, is in principle discoverable through rational enquiry. Moore seems to believe that a comparative and historical study of the moral orders and concrete forms of life expressed through the activities of men and women will eventually yield an authoritative standard of truth and justice. He does not, it should be added, claim to have finally discovered this standard. In fact he assumes that higher forms of rationality become possible with each stage of social evolution. His exploration of the utilitarian calculus of costs and benefits, to be discussed later in this book, provides him with an intellectual defence against ethical relativism while the larger objective described above is pursued. This strategy is reminiscent of the response of the philosophes to the weakening of their belief in the validity of natural law. Utilitarianism offered them an alternative intellectual and moral strategy.

Practical objectives

The final task of this chapter is to set out the practical objectives which Moore prescribes for social science, and especially for himself, in the 1950s. At the top of the list is the goal of 'finding principles of change that apply to more than a single series of events' (p.152). The professional group most clearly involved in the study of change in human affairs, the historians, have valuable techniques for tracing *particular* sequences of events. However, how could this knowledge of particulars be made susceptible to generalisation? Moore mentions the usual riposte of social scientists that 'we only understand the unique to the extent that we can analyse it into elements that are not unique' (p.146). However, he does not believe that generalisations should be imposed upon data through the arbitrary application of a system of universal categories in the head of the investigator. Instead the general may be found in the particular through acts of discovery. Moore believes that historical events which are unique in time and place and in several other respects may be aspects of general phenomena in three senses: first, some of them may be found to be manifestations of a general process in a specific society working itself out through several particular events over time; second, this process may occur in more than one society even though the particular events through which it is manifested are very different in several respects in the societies compared; and third, sequences of events in different societies may be manifestations of a single general process working itself out within a number of societies. As will be shown in Chapter 4, 'discoveries' of all three kinds were made in *Social Origins*. Paradoxically, the general processes which are found may well be unique to particular stages in social evolution. However, this is to anticipate the argument.

Despite the evolutionary undercurrents present in the theorising of a writer who admits the influence of both Hegel and Spencer (p.149; 1972, p.xii), we are not asked to accept any notion of the inexorable march of History. Social development is, in Moore's view, to an important degree subject to conscious human agency. This fact weakens the capacity of the social scientist to predict but at the same time it increases his moral responsibility because he should be able to outline the practical choices faced within societies. In Moore's opinion, the practice of social science is subject to an irreducible indeterminacy which has two aspects. First, processes which are understood when considered separately may interact with each other in ways which are not well understood. Furthermore, although study of the development of particular societies may produce a high level of understanding of their internal dynamics, the analyst may be left floundering if he tries to anticipate what will happen when societies come into contact with each other. Citing the early impact of the West upon Japan Moore comments: 'Certainly one could not have foretold what would have happened solely through an analysis of the processes at work in Japanese society alone nor, for that matter, in the West alone' (1955, p.114). In such cases understanding may be increased by retrospective examination of what actually occurred. Such reflection is likely to modify behaviour on subsequent occasions when apparently similar situations arise. The fact that behaviour may thus be modified in the light of experience and reason constitutes the second element of indeterminacy.

If the first task of social science, in Moore's view, is to reconcile the unique and the general, the second and equally important task is to distinguish between what is determined by historical or other constraining factors and what can be accomplished by actors themselves in human affairs. In other words, it has the task of specifying the real but limited options open to men and women in societies at particular stages in the development of those societies. This task should be performed both for the past and for the present:

> The main structural features of what society can be like in the next generation are already given by trends at work now. Humanity's freedom of manoeuvre lies within the framework created by history. Social scientists and allied scholars could help to widen the area of choice by analysing the historical trends that now limit it. They could show, impartially, honestly, and free from the special pleadings of governments and special interests, the range of possible alternatives and the potentialities for effective action. Such has been, after all, the aim of inquiry into human affairs since the Greeks. One may still hope that the tradition can survive in modern society. (Moore, 1958, p.159)

The limits within which choices have been made in history are, in Moore's opinion, to a considerable extent those imposed by the stage of evolution reached by a society and its neighbours at any one time. Moore is vigorously exploring in the 1950s various theoretical possibilities associated with the concept of social evolution. He finds it useful to distinguish between different stages of evolution according to the development of economic structure and technology and envisages 'a chronological series . . . from primitive hunting down to the large-scale bureaucratic firm'. Concepts such as 'stage-skipping' are found helpful as a possible means of analysing the rapid progress of Asian societies. Other intriguing notions are that certain societies might be the 'major vehicles' of each stage and that societies might experience bursts of rapid evolution and then become inhibited in their development like 'middle-aged tennis players' relying on 'a second-rate serve learned long ago' (p.153).

It is interesting to notice that this general line of thought was to produce not only *Social Origins* but also, published in the same year, Gerhard Lenski's *Power and Privilege*. There are, however, important differences between the way Moore and Lenski use evolutionary ideas. In Lenski's book universal propositions are illustrated with reference to a series of types of society: hunting and gathering, horticultural, agrarian, industrial. The procedure is heavily deductive, the object of illustrating theoretical generalisations being well to the fore. Technological innovations are seen as crucial, though not totally determining. One major deviation from this preoccupation is the role given to 'citizenship'. This is seen as a force for equality in industrial society which counteracts the tendency for economic surplus to be appropriated by the dominant class. *Social Origins* is much more inductive in emphasis and its author is concerned to explain processes of transformation between stages in particular cases. By comparison Lenski's treatment is much more static. Moore is far less prepared than Lenski to accept the overriding importance of technology. As Moore writes in 1958: 'New ideas may also play an equally important role' (p.154). His object is not the elaboration of theory as such but the elucidation of concrete historical processes. Furthermore, the problems of freedom, equality and justice in industrial societies are not, in Moore's eyes, to be disposed of by a relatively uncritical discussion of the extension of citizenship. In a sense Lenski's book, which has made a valuable contribution to the discussion of social development, represents the conclusion that Moore might have reached if he had continued along the path he was travelling in his early articles on social stratification and social control in the 1940s.

In fact, it will not do to label Moore an 'evolutionist' any more than it is acceptable to describe him as a 'latter-day philosophe'. So far two of the tasks he set for social science have been mentioned: to reconcile the unique and the general; and to identify the limits and range of choice in human affairs. There are two other tasks that have to be taken into account. These are, first, to distinguish between those aspects of society which recur through space and time, the constants of social life, from those aspects which manifest cumulative growth and change; and, second, to specify a workable procedure for making the moral choices which face men and women within the limits imposed both by history and by certain unchanging aspects of human societies and human nature.

3

Freedom and Necessity

Although Barrington Moore has been no one's disciple or apologist, it is interesting to notice the interplay between his work and that of Herbert Marcuse, a contemporary to whom he often refers warmly in his books. Both men were employed by the US Government during the Second World War, Moore as a political analyst in the Office of Strategic Studies and in the Department of Justice, Marcuse at the State Department in the Office of Intelligence Research where he became Acting Head of the East European section. Marcuse was later employed until 1954 at the Russian Research Centre at Harvard, an institution to which Moore has been attached for much of his working life. Marcuse's *Soviet Marxism* appeared in 1958, a few years after Moore's own work on Russia. In some respects, also, the essays in Moore's *Political Power and Social Theory* provide a response to suggestions made by Marcuse in another book, published three years previously, entitled *Eros and Civilization*. Similarly, Marcuse's *One-Dimensional Man*, which appeared in 1964, haunts the pages of *Reflections on the Causes of Human Misery* as a ghost to be laid, albeit with civility. Both men had contributed with R. P. Wolff to a small volume on tolerance in the late 1960s and at about the same time Moore co-edited a series of essays in honour of Marcuse.[1]

Marcuse, like Moore, has been deeply influenced by the writings of Hegel.[2] Both have been preoccupied with the themes of freedom, happiness, reason, tolerance, domination and truth. In a study of Marcuse's work, Alasdair MacIntyre has suggested that Marcuse's conceptual scheme derives not from an analysis of bourgeois society (since Marcuse is 'impatient of the empirical') but from a highly individual reading of Marx, Hegel and Freud (MacIntyre, 1970, pp.18, 40, 41). Since the present objective is to assess Moore, not Marcuse, comments will be restricted to pointing out some of the latter's arguments which are relevant here. First, Marcuse treats totalitarian societies, for example communist and fascist societies, as culminations of the development of bour-

geois capitalism. They stand not in opposition to bourgeois democratic societies but in the same camp as the latter. Second, the
future society to which Marcuse points is one in which freedom is
maximised, and as a consequence happiness becomes possible.
Third, the formal freedoms of bourgeois society disguise an
apparatus of repression which constrains and distorts even the
most intimate areas of human existence, including sexuality. In
less developed societies, repression and enforced conformity are a
necessary aspect of economic production, but this is not the case in
advanced bourgeois capitalism. The demands made in this society
upon its inhabitants extend far beyond those which are necessary
to produce the material comforts of civilisation. Oppressive techniques for producing conformity maintain a social order in being
which denies the possibility of happiness for its members.

In *Political Power and Social Theory*, Moore includes essays on
the processes by which political power is acquired and maintained,
the use of totalitarian techniques in pre-industrial societies, the
future of the family and, finally, the elements of conformity in
industrial society. The implicit questions running through these
essays are as follows: Which elements of the social order in contemporary industrial societies are unique and necessary to those
societies? Which elements are shared with other types of society,
possibly because they belong to a limited range of workable solutions to problems encountered in very similar forms in more than
one type of society? And which elements of industrial society
commonly assumed to be necessary are in fact not necessary and
could disappear without leading to that society's destruction? The
subjects chosen by Moore and the way in which he treats them
allow him not only to develop an implicit critique of Marcuse's
position but also to pursue the further objective of distinguishing
the constant from the variable elements of human societies.

Constants and variables

In his 'Notes on the process of acquiring power' Moore presents a
brilliant *tour de force* which encompasses 'the Bolsheviks on the
way to the Kremlin, the early Christians on the route that leads to
Innocent III, the French kings on the road to Versailles, the
Moguls on the way to the splendours of Shah Jahan's reign' (1958,

p.2). He distinguishes three situations likely to occur in any relatively complex society which tend to stimulate 'an active search for political power and centralization' (p.2). The situations are: the acquisition of new activities in a society requiring central co-ordination; external shock or internal decay stimulating a demand for change; and the recognition and exploitation of the potential for domination over a loosely ordered system by one segment of it (pp.2–3). The last situation encourages a process of gradual consolidation of power which Moore labels 'monarchical absolutism'.

Moore also specifies a limited number of strategies that power-seekers may adopt and the problems which these strategies entail. Power-seekers may articulate widespread discontent with the society's failure to meet the expectations of its members through the means of a 'charter myth' or political doctrine. The charter myth is likely to express either 'nativism' or 'xenophilia' in its attitude to the culture of its own and other societies. With respect to the disposition of wealth, political power and status, it may be either 'egalitarian' or 'hierarchical'. Clearly four combinations are possible in principle. However, Moore pays particular attention to charter myths combining nativism and hierarchy (e.g. fascism) and those combining nativism and egalitarianism (e.g. communism under certain conditions). He stresses that political tensions are created by contradictions within and between the ideological components of these charter myths. Furthermore, although the latter may determine by their logic how authority shall be allocated within power-seeking organisations, once a leader acquires a high degree of centralised control within the organisation he or she may be able to alter important aspects of the charter myth itself.

Three possible modes of control and co-ordination within the power-seeking organisation are distinguished, each with its own particular problems. Feudalism, which coheres through diffuse relationships, does not permit a central policy to be enforced through its hierarchy. Rational bureaucracy overcomes this but at the expense of undertaking the destruction of the old order. Totalitarianism elicits obedience by gaining total commitment from subordinates and acquires flexibility by dispensing with fixed bureaucratic rules. However, the cost of such a strategy is that the leader has to be far better informed than in a rational bureaucracy about behaviour at all hierarchical levels and has to insist upon acting as arbiter in all cases of dispute, however trivial. Feudalism entails the allocation of control over resources to subordinates without a close specification or monitoring of subordinates' functions. Rational bureaucracy entails the allocation of specific functions to subordinates as well as delegation to them of control over necessary resources. Totalitarianism entails the allocation and strict monitoring of functions without the delegation of control over resources. The three forms are not historical stages since each form contains contradictions tending to transform it into one or both of the other forms.

Turning to the relationship between the power-seeking organisations and the external environment within which legitimacy and power are sought, Moore argues that four problems are faced: Should a mass following be sought or a close-knit body of supporters forged? To what extent can tactical alliances be made with other groups without creating a threat to the organisation's identity and programme? When power has been achieved, to what extent is opposition to be tolerated or power shared? And is the structure of the society to be transformed or left as it is? Solutions to these problems are determined both by the internal structure of the power-seeking organisation and by the structure of the wider society. The latter only is discussed, the crucial distinctions being three: whether the society is stable or unstable; whether the legitimacy of the status quo is widely accepted or not by the general population; and whether authority is centralised or not within the society.

In cases where the legitimacy of the status quo is accepted and authority is quite widely diffused through the social structure the power-seeking organisation is liable to make many alliances, tolerate opposition and not seek fundamental social reform (e.g. American society around 1900). In a stable society with highly centralised or despotic authority, the possibility of carrying out a palace revolution eliminates the need of the power-seeking organisation for a mass following or numerous alliances (as opposed to passive acquiescence by potential opponents). By contrast, a decaying social order, perhaps experiencing the impact of industrialisation, offers opportunities for building up a mass clientele susceptible to a nativist or egalitarian charter myth. 'Such movements are likely to develop totalitarian features' (p.26). Shunning compromising alliances, a totalitarian organisation will use political power to restructure the social order and capture as much control as possible over all social activities.

Having outlined the limited range of problems and solutions available to power-seeking organisations (though without claiming to have provided 'a complete theory of power') Moore argues that 'at least four discernible processes of acquiring power' may be identified which 'take their essential pattern from the way in which the process begins' (p.27). The first is the totalitarian pattern, stimulated by either an external shock to the society or internal decay. In this case the charter myth of the power-seeking organisation tends to acquire an hierarchical emphasis over time despite its initial egalitarianism. Where decay or fragmentation has become more advanced in a society, a pattern of monarchical absolutism is possible. This second pattern tends to exhibit a mixture of bureaucratic rationality and totalitarian control but in important ways the power-seekers compromise with the *status quo ante*. Third, the rise of new activities such as industrial production may be associated with either egalitarian or hierarchical charter myths depending upon the degree of congruence between the new activities and established wants and dispositions. Finally, feudalism as a power-seeking strategy may emerge in conditions of fragmentation and generate a hierarchical charter myth stressing diffuse sanctions which limit the forms of future growth. These various forms 'appear to be recurring subpatterns within the over-all process of irreversible historical development that characterises human society as a whole'. In any given epoch one would expect to find 'an emphasis upon one of these forms combined with a subordinate utilisation of the others' (p.29).

This paper has been examined at length for a number of reasons. It exemplifies the significance Moore attaches to continually recurring cycles of similar structure within a broad evolutionary scheme. It also illustrates the part he believes is played by ideas, in this case charter myths, in making a relatively autonomous contribution to transformations in the social order. Processes of differentiation within crucial social movements may be partly explained, he believes, by the need to sustain legitimacy and identity within a given ideological framework. The development of particular charter myths is explained in terms of a response to contradictions arising from established wants which are not being met within the existing social order. Moore's Hegelianism is evident here (pp.10–11). This paper, which is an important bridge between his earlier work on Russia and his later project, *Social Origins*, also emphasises that major transformations in societies may derive from deliberate human efforts to solve problems. In this case Moore stresses the limits imposed upon these efforts by two factors: the invariant characteristics of the finite range of organisational forms which may be employed to co-ordinate the behaviour of large numbers of human beings; and the restrictions and opportunities existing within complex social orders according to their degrees of centralisation, integration and legitimacy. Moore finds that variations can occur within this range of possibilities independently of the stage of social development, in technology or other respects, reached by a society.

Functionalism and evolutionism

The other papers will be discussed more briefly. In 'Totalitarian elements in pre-industrial societies' Moore uses the word 'totalitarian' to refer to societies within which a large number of activities are directed through coercion or repression. Coercion may be exercised either from a single political centre or through 'a decentralised and diffuse system accepted by the mass of the population' (pp.31–2). Adopting a strategy in some respects similar to that subsequently used in the early chapters of *Injustice*, Moore reports on a search for examples of totalitarian practices in societies varying widely in time, space and level of development.

Moore's findings contradict Marcuse's assumptions that totalitarianism is a particular response to the contradictions of bourgeois capitalism. They also throw doubt upon the notion that repression in pre-industrial societies might be wholly explained by the requirements of the economic system. Three main empirical findings are reported. The first is that 'diffuse conformity to repressive and irrational standards of behaviour' occurred in preliterate societies, especially in witchcraft practices. Such practices are seen by Moore as a response to problems for which the cultures concerned have no solution. Aggression is released by victimising individuals or groups who are held to be responsible for the social ills. In a fine passage of cosmic pessimism Moore draws a parallel with Nazi genocide, Stalin's purges and McCarthyism, characterising these movements as a kind of bureaucratised witchcraft (p.39). Second, investigation of the Ch'ing dynasty (221–209 BC) suggests that many of the institutional forms and ideological justifications of centralised totalitarianism, with its spy system, book-burning and contempt for the masses, were to be found in ancient China as well as contemporary Russia. Finally, in six-teenth-century Geneva the disintegration of a delicate balance between competing political, economic and religious interests gen-erated social instability and widespread anxiety. In the develop-ment of this situation 'economic conflicts did not play a major role' (p.63). A single-minded religious group headed by Calvin was able to achieve power and enforce a set of beliefs and institutions which imposed religious controls upon the inhabitants. The Consisto-rium, which 'performed the service of a secret police and moral censorship', showed 'many striking parallels to modern practices' (p.70). It is clear from his discussion that Moore sympathises with the Marcusian line that a 'sham democracy' may give the illusion of freedom and equality while denying its substance. However, Moore has found these techniques being implemented in Geneva, a pre-industrial society, 'Without an attempt to control the econ-omy' (p.76).

In his 'Thoughts on the future of the family' Moore reverses his strategy and presents arguments to the effect that the institution of the family, whose universal necessity was 'almost axiomatic', might well 'be an obsolete institution or become one before long' (pp.160–1). He suggests that the family might well be a hangover from a pre-industrial age, 'a repressive survival under the condi-tions of advanced technology':

> The exploitation of socially sanctioned demands for gratitude, when the existing social situation no longer generates any genu-ine feeling of warmth, is a subtle and heavily tabooed result of this barbaric heritage. (Moore, 1958, p.164)

So much for motherly love! In Moore's opinion, influence and authority have been syphoned away from parents to institutions outside the family. The media have 'destroyed the flow of private communications within the family that were once the basis of socialisation' (p.166). Motherhood cramps the personality. Ado-lescence is a torment because of the contradiction between family values and those of the adult world. An institutional environment might be capable of providing more warmth and support than resentful parents. In brief, the current state of the family, Moore claims, is that of an institution losing its traditional functions and probably doomed to extinction.

Having pitted evolutionary ideas against functionalism, Moore proceeds, in the next paper to be discussed, to exploit functionalist arguments as a means of combatting the Marcusian assertion that there is a necessary connection between industrialism and totalitarianism. His object in 'Reflections on conformity in industrial society' is to find out 'the minimum content of conformity necessary to make an industrial society work', a task he sharply distinguishes from that of assessing 'the probable future of industrial society' (pp.179, 180, 181). His answers fall under 'five rough-and-ready empirical headings' (p.186). First, conformity is needed with 'the basic logical principles of the world around us'. Second, appreciation of and, by implication, participation in a culture requires disciplined effort by individuals to learn its rules, procedures and assumptions. Third, conformity with managerial decisions concerning the production and allocation of resources is necessary. Fourth, conformity to a degree of social control is needed to cope with 'basically selfish, aggressive, and evil tendencies in biological human nature'. Finally, there must be conformity to some set of 'non-empirical beliefs'. Moore reaches this last conclusion on the basis that 'all known human societies' have shown some such attachment to non-empirical beliefs and this has 'in the past provided one of the main bases of social cohesion' (pp.186–8). It is apparent that this list of requirements would apply to many complex societies, perhaps any society, and not simply to industrial societies.

It is now possible to summarise the conclusions Moore reaches in *Political Power and Social Theory* about the constants and variable aspects of human societies. First, he argues that certain institutions or practices considered to be unique to industrial societies, such as totalitarian techniques, are in fact not unique to such societies. Second, he argues that certain institutions thought necessary to industrial societies, such as the family, may in fact not be necessary. Third, he specifies certain types of institution and practice which are necessary because of the functional contribution they make to a society's survival. Finally, he identifies certain recurrent cycles of human activity and institutional change in the political sphere, found both in industrial societies and other complex societies. The characteristics of these cycles derive from the structural limits, potentialities and dilemmas intrinsic to the institutional forms through which complex social networks may be coordinated. They are also affected by given levels of centralisation, integration and legitimacy within social orders.

During the late 1950s, as he is presumably working his way deep into the empirical data which were to be the basis of *Social Origins*, Moore has a theoretical position of fascinating complexity. He begins, like the philosophes, by acknowledging the responsibility of men and women to make rational moral choices on the basis of a clear-sighted understanding of the facts. Moore then finds in Hegel a perspective which stresses the critical function of reason in society, the part played by reason in processes of historical development and, furthermore, the limits imposed by each stage of historical development upon the choices that can be made. As a result of his own empirical work, Moore does not share Hegel's confidence that succeeding epochs *necessarily* manifest a progressive unfolding of reason and its concrete manifestation to an increasing extent in instititions expressing ever-higher principles of freedom (1958, pp.39, 188).

However, Moore regards the position to which Marcuse's work leads as being one of 'mere peevishness about the present', which is treated as being totally repressive, combined with 'sheer optimism about the future' which is envisaged as being a realm of complctc freedom (p.180). Neither opinion seems to Moore to owe much to reason or empirical enquiry. He distances himself, theoretically, from Marcuse by borrowing from the functionalist tradition in order to specify the minimum functional requisites of society. In this way he is able to determine the minimum degree of enforced conformity which is necessary in industrial society and, perhaps, in all societies. Beyond this sphere 'necessity' has to be demonstrated through empirical enquiry into the constraints imposed upon particular societies by the fact that sequences of historical development have closed off certain options and opened up others. As an orienting device in this enquiry he adopts an evolutionary perspective, thus distancing himself theoretically from the functionalist school with their equilibrium model (1955, pp.111–12).

However, Moore's own historical work on political change has led him to recognise recurrent patterns in the political sphere which manifest themselves in similar form in successive evolutionary stages (1955, p.113). This perspective enables Moore to distance himself, theoretically, from a rigid evolutionism, especially one which assumes the overall determining effect of technological development. Finally, Moore has by this time developed an approach to political ideologies which asserts that they crystallise in the context of frustrated expectations experienced by social groups, and that this frustration might in some cases be due to causes which do not originate in the mode of production. He also suggests that collective belief in ideologies has a range of possible consequences for social differentiation and that these consequences have an orderly nature which is discoverable by reason and empirical enquiry.[3]

This finely tuned theoretical position expressed a balance between a desire for intellectual order, fidelity to the facts and a determination to keep the door to moral choice wedged firmly open. As a working scholar's compromise it clearly sufficed, providing the heuristic guide which made the writing of *Social Origins* possible. However, did it provide a moral guide which would enable men and women to assess contemporary society and make choices tending to bring into being a society which was happy, just and free? Did it specify the correct sphere and limits of a 'necessary' repression whose function within society was to create the conditions of justice and freedom? In 1958 Moore regretfully acknowledged that moral choices had to be made without absolute certainty. In the late 1960s and early 1970s, with *Social Origins* behind him, he turned to the above questions more directly.

Reason and anger

If, as the story goes, Hegel's *Phenomenology of Mind* was finished with the sound of Napoleon's guns at the battle of Jena in the author's ears, then *Social Origins* must have been completed to the sound of police sirens and breaking glass. In 'Thoughts on violence', published in 1968, Moore has no hesitation in exposing as a deceptive myth the belief that American society has moderate and pragmatic objectives which justify 'the terrifying violence in which American democracy now engages'. In fact, he argues, 'the predominant voice of America at home and abroad has become the voice of white racism' (1968, p.2). However, although Moore has an evident capacity to make words blister the page, this aspect of his style is not given untrammelled license. As he writes in a later preface, 'the mere expression of anger is in my judgement light work' (1972, p.xvi). The harder and more necessary task is to employ 'sound reasoning and evidence' in the search for truths which are relevant to 'human needs and purposes' (1969b, pp.67, 68). It has to be recognised also that although this search might be governed by the political concerns of intellectuals, 'the truths they uncover may often be and actually are extremely damaging to exactly these concerns' (p.90).[4]

Within a broadly unchanged intellectual and moral strategy, three changes of emphasis may be recognised when the essays published after *Social Origins* are compared with those which preceded it. First, there is a new determination to expose political mythology as fraud, recalling in some respects Bentham's attack on 'fictions'.[5] In 'The society nobody wants: a look beyond Marxism and Liberalism', which appeared in 1967, Moore considers the radical critique of American capitalism and the liberal critique of communism. Radical critics, Moore argues, fail to provide evidence that imperialist traits are uniquely characteristic of modern capitalist societies and hence could be removed by changing those institutions that are specific to post-war America. Pre-capitalist societies and earlier capitalist societies both displayed similar imperialist traits. Moore has to dismiss the case on grounds of logic and evidence (1967, pp.404, 406–7). The liberal critique of communist society fails to demonstrate the necessity of its basic assumption that political pluralism is never oppressive whereas bureaucracy always is. Both critiques derive from doctrines, Marxism and Liberalism, which have 'in good measure ceased to provide explanations of the world' (p.418).

This paper also illustrates a second development in Moore's work: a greater confidence in making generalisations about human nature. For example, 'Human beings have rather more difficulties in agreeing upon what they do want than what they do not want' (p.401); 'Human beings show . . . a tremendous capacity to put up with hardship and danger when they really want something' (p.408); 'The great mass of the population most of the time in most countries . . . display yearnings for a peaceful world, and definitely one without poverty or gross injustice' (p.409); the good citizen always has a 'reluctance to jeopardize his stake in the prevailing order' (pp.411–12). Behind these statements lies a confidence presumably grounded in the accumulated evidence collected during the decade of work on *Social Origins*, a process of empirical enquiry which Moore's general position would suggest is the necessary basis, in conjunction with reason, for arriving at such generalisations. The implication is that they are not mere *a priori* assertions and cannot be legitimately opposed with *a priori* denials but only with reason and evidence. In effect, Moore has resumed the ambitious empirical and historical enquiry which was begun in the first part of Adam Ferguson's *Essay on the History of Civil Society* entitled 'Of the general characteristics of human nature'.

According to Moore certain persisting traits in human nature help account for repeated cycles, found in Rome and Greece as much as in contemporary America, such as that 'Recurring historical phenomenon: the repeated failure of human societies to come anywhere near the type of decent society that was perhaps within their reach at a given stage of development' (p.409). The reluctance of citizens to risk their existing stake in a given order, however unjust and repressive, is a constant human characteristic. It is encouraged by certain invariant features of social relations. For example, an offer to co-operate with others in order to change the system runs the risk of non-reciprocation: 'the dilemma of the first move' (p.411). The constant risk that others will make you their prey encourages aggression by all. In fact, 'something resembling Gresham's law is always at work in politics. At any given moment there exists a strong temptation to establish a predatory society.'[6] Moore concludes that such tendencies go a long way towards explaining popular acquiescence in any given social order, providing 'the pillars of the community' with 'impregnable justifications for the unhappiness they cause others' (p.412).

A third shift of emphasis in Moore's work, at which the last phrase hints, is the adoption of a tactic of '*reculer pour mieux sauter*' in the grand enterprise of moral critique. In the late 1950s he had come up against an apparently impassible barrier when attempting to specify the institutional arrangements which would make a society 'free' and, by implication, 'happy' and 'just' (1958 p.195). The prospect he envisaged was of the intellectual having 'to go down with his ship, with all banners flying and steam hissing from the boilers, on behalf of principles about which absolute certainty is impossible' (p.196). By the late 1960s a life-boat, or at least a life-belt, is at hand. Instead of the pursuit of happiness, freedom and justice, Moore turns his attention to the avoidance of misery, intolerance and oppression. By concentrating on forms of suffering produced by societies which people universally do not want and which, furthermore, they tend to agree they do not want, he can undertake an enquiry whose moral criteria are to that extent self-evident. He can concentrate upon the task of demonstrating that many forms of human misery are neither necessary nor unavoidable despite the contrary assumptions of prevailing ideologies and 'common sense'.

Moore's justification for undertaking this task is that 'The evidence is reasonably clear that human beings do not want a life of suffering, at least for its own sake' (1972, p.5). In a sense, by attempting to think clearly about the half-articulated desires of ordinary people with respect to the societies in which they live, to draw out their implications rationally and to indicate the obstacles in the way of their achievement, Moore is engaging in the task which Hegel assigned to the philosopher in any age. From such a perspective, Moore is helping to heighten consciousness as a prelude to an epoch of elevated reason and increased moral responsibility in a transformed society. It should be noted that Moore assumes a kind of 'professional pessimism' about such a prospect. However, practical judgements have to be made, he believes, about which aspects of misery are unnecessary in principle and what prospects there are for changing them in fact.

Three procedures are appropriate for this task. First, the 'prerequisites of human existence' have to be determined, in other words the resources and activities without which society is impossible. To establish what they are 'is no task to be performed once and for all. It changes with historical conditions' (1969b, p.80). Second, it has to be shown that 'existing facts contain the potential of becoming something different from what they are' (p.81). This is possible through careful empirical and logical analysis. The third procedure, essential to the moral enterprise, is to undertake as scientific an assessment as is possible of the likely costs and benefits of, on the one hand, acquiescing in existing arrangements and, on the other hand, engaging in various attempts to alter them. As early as 1955 Moore had stressed the sociologist's duty of 'outlin-

ing the range of possibilities for the future and the costs of alternative policies' (1955, p.115). Seventeen years later this principle
stands at the centre of Moore's moral calculus.

Misery and happiness

At the beginning of *Anna Karenina* Tolstoy declares: 'All happy
families are alike but an unhappy family is unhappy after its own
fashion' (1954, p.13). In *Reflections on the Causes of Human
Misery and on Certain Proposals to Eliminate Them*, to give the
book its full evocative title, Barrington Moore finds that a discussion of personal unhappiness such as that due to disappointment in
love is outside his immediate concerns (1972, p.xvi). In this book
he develops an approach to the misery due to 'institutional causes'
which contradicts Tolstoy's epigram. In Moore's view, the origins
and characteristics of happiness are infinite when compared with
'the unity of misery' (1972, p.11). In a rough-and-ready way
Moore divides the causes of human suffering into four categories:
war; poverty, hunger and disease; injustice and oppression; persecution for beliefs.

Moore's objective is to make a start towards providing a social
analysis which will enable moral objectives to be pursued through
political action in the light of a rational assessment of likely costs
and benefits. Moral objectives are intrinsic to politics since these
concern the ways human beings are to be treated as means and
ends (pp.3, 10). Three problems arise. First, costs and benefits
may be difficult to predict in certain circumstances. This, argues
Moore, is an irreducible difficulty that affects all participants in
politics. Rational analysis on the basis of all available knowledge
is, however, the indispensable preliminary to action – or inaction
(1972, pp.9, 10; 1969a, p.89). Second, it may be objected that
costs and benefits (and by the latter Moore seems to mean a
reduction of costs in this context) are not truly commensurable
between societies and time periods. Moore's answer is 'that a
general opposition to human suffering constitutes a standpoint
that both transcends and unites different cultures and historical
epochs' (1972, p.11). He does not provide a way of choosing
between alternative costs (e.g. hunger *vs* oppression) but focuses
rather upon variations in the level of the whole bundle of costs

between groups and over time. A third problem concerns the fact that people may 'feel happy under oppressive circumstances' (p.12). Moore argues that although people 'make the best of it' when suffering is regarded as not being due to human agency, their perceptions of suffering, its causes and potential cures, becomes more secular over time:

> As men gained control over the physical aspects of their environment, secular explanations eventually permeated the understanding of social and political affairs even if they did not yield in social affairs the same degree of control. (Moore, 1972, p.12)

Moore argues that such understandings or perceptions affect the degree to which people are prepared to 'make the best of it' and provide a means of identifying friend and foe; they are 'the emotional and intellectual bases of politics'. Liberalism and communism are the last in 'a long historical chain' of successive diagnoses.

In the second essay, entitled 'Of war, cruelty, oppression and general human nastiness', Moore's basic proposition is that warfare between societies and cruelty within them are to be understood as being in large measure the products of acts intended to maintain, extend or bring into existence social orders embodying particular moral principles of human organisation. Material interests alone are insufficient to account for the irreconcilability between groups and persons which produces these acts (p.22). Moore also discusses a further category of 'nasty' or 'immoral' behaviour which involves the evasion of principles of moral obligation rather than attempts to impose or defend such principles.

A distinction is made between forms of cruelty and conflict which 'are part of the way most, and perhaps all social orders work' and those which are 'conflicts over who should rule and by what rules' (p.31). The latter entail the deliberate infliction of pain for a purpose. Given that few people would call competent and effective surgery cruel, it is evident that in some cases the infliction of pain is justified. At this point the discussion concerns the deliberate bringing about of suffering which is not 'necessary'; in other words, if the acts concerned did not take place, society would not as a consequence cease to exist. According to Moore, certain criteria should be applied to such acts. First, their purpose should be to reduce suffering in the long run. Second, they should be carried out in accordance with the best knowledge available. Third, the future benefits intended to be produced should not be delayed too long. Fourth, there should be a reasonable likelihood of success, given the likely costs of failure. Moore mentions some of the difficulties this scheme involves. For example, how do we assess, in terms of justifiability, acts which were based upon the 'best knowledge available' at the time in cases where this knowledge is later judged to be myth? The Inquisition is one such example. Furthermore, how long a time is to elapse before a comparative assessment of costs and benefits is made? A generation? A century? The case of the French Revolution is relevant here (pp.26–7, 29).

The other broad class of violent or conflictual acts discussed are those endemic to social life. They are inevitable and probably necessary, believes Moore, who suspects 'that human cooperation is impossible without some sort of hostile and resisting target' (p.32).[7] In the international sphere conflict need not be explained in terms of an aggressive instinct but is a consequence of the unavoidable insecurities produced within a system of sovereign powers. Their behaviour is imposed upon participants by the structure of the international system. Warfare and destruction are built-in structural tendencies within an arena which, while not subject to moral regulation, manifests observable cycles and trends. As in the market, a similar system in many respects, rational behaviour by individual members may produce collective irrationality. It is structurally much more difficult to modify the irrationality in the international sphere than within particular societies. In the latter case the state may regulate the effects of the market but no equivalent global institution has comparable powers in the international sphere.

Moore argues that the system of political relations among states has had a more powerful effect, globally, than the free market of competitive capitalism whose influence has been restricted in time and space: 'Can one therefore point to sanctions that transcend the workings of industrial society that explain the ubiquity of mutual destruction?' (p.35). Moore's affirmative answer is that foreign conquest would damage whatever stake people have in their own social order, a stake which has been greatly increased for ordinary people by the industrial revolution. The consequences of an inevitable insecurity in relations between states are therefore fundamental.

Within particular societies violence and more peaceful forms of rule-breaking are, in the short run, effective means of obtaining advantages, though they cannot in themselves provide the basis of social order. Given the effectiveness of violent and deceitful behaviour, there is a structural tendency for its adoption to become more widespread in the political sphere. Such acts are treated by Moore as being an inevitable feature of social life, a form of unavoidable cost. He identifies a 'fundamental contradiction between the effectiveness of immoral political methods and the necessity for morality in any social order' (p.38). It is a contradiction faced above all, he argues, by revolutionaries who typically resort to immoral means such as violence and deceit in order to establish their own new moral order.

In the following essay, 'Of hunger, toil, injustice and oppression', he deals with two interconnected issues. These are, first, the structural sources of scarcity and the costs of trying to counteract them, and second, the structural and moral implications of various forms of political domination and the implications of attempts by varying means to reduce the costs of these forms of domination. Moore begins by pointing out that progress towards eliminating scarcity and increasing individual autonomy through technological progress is counteracted by two tendencies: the rapid increase in world population which negates the former, and the need to extend the scope of bureaucratic regulation in order to cope with growing social density which negates the latter (pp.41–4). Furthermore, conceptions of scarcity and necessity are subject to continual upward revision due to political competition within and between societies (p.47). Reversal of these tendencies through de-industrialisation would entail massive suffering and widespread death. A likely outcome would be the establishment of an authoritarian world dictatorship to co-ordinate production and exchange and enforce a downward revision of cultural expectations. The costs would probably be greater than the benefits. A single central authority could only be avoided if the conditions for peaceful exchange between independent states existed, i.e. if these states were of roughly equal size and if exchange partners internalised the rules of the game including the acceptance of sanctions for 'wrong moves'. Moore doubts that a necessarily disruptive process of de-industrialisation would be likely to generate these latter conditions. In the absence of catastrophe the future he envisages is one in which human life becomes 'more organized and controlled, less "authentic", spontaneous, independent and anarchic' (p.51).

Turning to the examination of political domination, he discusses the criteria which should be used to judge the rationality of political authority and the institutional means by which sanctions may be applied to rulers. He argues that the principles of rationality by which the legitimacy of rulers should be judged are in fact implicit within 'a common substratum of universal human feelings that one can call the sense of injustice'. These feelings derive directly from 'The experience of living in society' and include a sense of whether or not particular forms of suffering have 'justifications within the routine of social life' with its recurring activities, division of labour and life cycles (p.52). Moore believes that systems of legitimate or rational authority express, are judged and should be judged according to three criteria. First, the ruler must pursue political goals which tend to reduce human misery. Second, the ruler must be competent according to available means and standards of assessment. In this respect, Moore notes that over time modes of assessment and forms of knowledge change, eliciting shifts in the locus of authority, for example 'from medicineman, shaman, and rain maker to the modern metereologist and doctor' (p.56). Third, a reciprocity must exist between the obedience of subordinates and those services provided by the ruler which contribute to the welfare of the group. The content and meaning of reciprocity are transformed in the course of social evolution (p.55). However, it is always possible in principle to distinguish between genuine reciprocity and violations of this principle through 'pseudo-reciprocity', excessive compulsion or misuse of resources drawn from subordinates. 'Exploitation' occurs in cases where over a range of exchanges the goods and services exchanged are of radically unequal value and one party uses a substantial degree of coercion (p.53).

Confronting the issue of how to control authority, Moore first makes the general point that although political change has in large part been the result of violence, this means 'by itself is ineffective'. Contributions have also been made by government action, changes in the mode of production and 'the slow ferment of critical ideas' (p.61). He then assesses the costs and benefits of various systems of rule which claim to have 'self-correcting mechanisms against the irrational abuse of authority' (p.62). Moore indicates the benefits of a roughly equal distribution of property, the latter term being defined broadly to include the resources, including material wealth, education and occupational skills, possessed by a person which enable him to have self-respect and a capacity to veto some decisions made by those in authority. Such a prospect is contrary to current trends, he notes, but 'these trends are not irreversible' (p.63). A further possibility is an oligarchic system in which competing elites have an interest in exposing and preventing abuses by their opponents on behalf of 'the public interest'. An oligarchy might, Moore believes, contribute to the development of a rational society through the transmission of 'a certain cast of mind and a set of intellectual skills' within families possessing political and other kinds of authority over a number of generations (pp.63–4). Such an outcome would be preferable, in Moore's view, to the destructive resentment of the failures in a society with complete equality of opportunity.

Moore then considers the options of direct democracy and participatory democracy including industrial self-management. The first, history shows, leads to revolutionary terror. The second may only operate within limited spheres, the important decisions being taken by central authority. In any case, adds Moore, committees impose suffering upon their members! 'A very precious part of human freedom is that *not* to take decisions' (p.69). A committee-ridden system of parliamentary democracy is likely in practice to be clogged with trivial issues and in principle to be unable to furnish peaceful resolutions of profound moral disagreements about how society should be run (pp.68–9). Furthermore, socialist revolutionaries have no better answers to the problem of *quis custodiet custodes*? Marxism, Moore believes, provides no answer to the questions of how political succession will occur, how shifts in policy will be justified or how the people will be protected from the abuses of their rulers. Finally, proposals for the elimination of all centralised authority ignore the potentially enormous costs of the absence of order and the great likelihood of violent conflict between the local communities envisaged within the anarchist model. Also ignored are the probable emergence of a class of 'operators', traders or 'fixers', whose existence would tend to subvert the desired order, and the likelihood that a new central authority would appear in response to these dilemmas.

Having reached these dismal conclusions, Moore decides that there is a pressing need for more 'free intellectual inquiry' to enable us to advance beyond them. In 'Of heresy, intellectual freedom and scholarship', Moore focuses directly upon the need to *improve* rationality rather than upon the task of applying reason in its *existing* stage of development to the assessment of potential means of reducing misery. Having devoted many pages to a description of evils, Moore now identifies his own conception of 'the good' which turns out to be 'the disinterested pursuit of truth and beauty', a quest to be undertaken 'irrespective of the consequences' (p.93). However, Moore recognises an unavoidable requirement to compromise this pursuit with, first, the other imperatives of the moral calculus already developed by him, second, the constraints deriving from any social order in which intellectual activity takes place, and, third, the particular constraints associated with contemporary industrial society.

Effective inquiry into the causes of misery, obstacles to the reduction of misery, and the possibilities and costs of eliminating these obstacles, requires intellectual freedom as an essential means. The disinterested pursuit of truth as an end in itself also necessarily implies intellectual freedom. Two questions may be asked. Should some aspects of this desired freedom be regarded as obstacles to or a diversion from the pursuit of the reduction of misery and oppression, and thus be restricted? To what extent should the objective of reducing misery be disregarded in favour of other values? Moore acknowledges the possibility, perhaps the likelihood, that intellectual inquiry might produce knowledge which undermines beliefs which support the moral intention of reducing misery. However, he thinks that inconvenient facts should be discovered if possible so that any feasible avoiding action may be taken. Further, it is impossible to know in advance whether new knowledge will be favourable or unfavourable to specific moral positions (pp.79–81). Finally, philosophies incongruent with the pursuit of a reduction in misery should be permitted since the basis of rationality is strengthened through argument (pp.81–3).

Having defended the practice of intellectual freedom against

potential objections arising from a particular utilitarian standpoint, Moore sets out the conditions which are ideally necessary
for a society 'to permit full and free discussion of any and all sorts
of viewpoints on all subjects' (p.84). Accepting the need to forbid
the use of technical means for 'primarily destructive purposes' on
grounds of irrationality (p.81). Moore lists his other requirements.
The society would be free from foreign danger. Its inhabitants
would be emotionally secure, rational and possess the technical
and intellectual competence provided by a broad and coherent
liberal education. A rough socio-economic equality would inhibit
the appearance of a powerful establishment controlling thought.
There would, however, be informal controls over the rate of
intellectual innovation (in order to protect moral stability) and
also over the direction of research investment. Control in both
these areas would, presumably, be based upon a rational consensus. In such a society, as in all societies, intellectual activity would
'reflect in large measure the interests and conceptions of the
dominant groups in society' (p.86) – hence the vital importance of
the particular disposition of social influence and rational attitudes
outlined above.

The contingent obstacles to such a society in the modern world
are the unequal distribution of wealth and power within societies
and the 'recurring imperatives of international politics' (p.88).
Two further obstacles inherent in all societies are, first, the limited
amount of intellectual resources available, requiring a direction of
thought towards a limited range of purposes, and, second, the
apparently inescapable need to ground moral sentiments in a set
of non-rational and non-calculative responses such as 'horror'
(p.88). Moore concentrates on the institutional means available to
cope with the contradiction between, on the one hand, the need to
control intellectual speculation and innovation as a means of pro-
tecting a society's moral order and, on the other hand, the need to
maximise it in order to allow rationality to progress through the
pursuit of truth. He argues that a strong bias towards the latter
objective has been given by the relative success of efforts 'that go
back at least twenty-five centuries' in favour of the right of legitimate opposition to authority (p.89). This historical trend has in
different epochs owed its force to various groups, notably the
aristocracy. The bourgeois contribution to this trend, though important, has not been the only one.

The contradiction between the pressures towards moral stability on the one hand and intellectual innovation on the other are managed within a number of intellectual spheres, but Moore concentrates on only one: the university. Despite its 'elitism, hypocrisy and make-believe' (p.92), the university endeavours to make intellectual criticism and innovation a regular and acceptable activity at the necessary cost of some degree of detachment from society. This detachment enables the university to institutionalise the rules of intellectual freedom and open debate. Such conditions should permit all opinions, however obnoxious or however passionately held, to be heard and subjected to the test of rational criticism. However, Moore also argues that the university should impose upon itself 'a coherent intellectual strategy' (p.100) on the basis not of political demands for 'relevance' but more rational considerations. The obligations upon the academic intellectual are: to analyse the causes of violence and the threats to freedom in the current social order; to avoid becoming the voice of any particular class or interest group; to be aware that the knowledge discovered has political implications; to 'distinguish between serious argument and specious rationalization'; and, finally, to give 'a large space to the search for truth that widens human horizons in time and space and for the beauty that enriches it' (p.103). In doing so the intellectual should not only be aware that this activity has costs for others but also should make efforts to see that such costs do not fall on those least able to bear them.

Unresolved dilemmas

Reflections on the Causes of Human Misery may be understood on at least three levels. Superficially, the book considers four causes of human misery – violence, material deprivation, unjust oppression and persecution for heretical beliefs – in order to assess the practical possibilities of eliminating them. However, as will be evident from the preceding account, Moore's discussion of these topics is rather diffuse and does not lead to a strong positive conclusion. In fact, the simplicity of the book's formal structure disguises a more complex analysis which concludes that many of the 'causes' of human misery are endemic in social relationships and cannot be 'eliminated'. At this second level it emerges that the causes of human misery include the following factors: conflicts arising from moral disagreements about the principles which should be expressed within political orders; competition between individuals, groups and societies in the course of modernisation (which has the effect of continually revising upwards the prevailing definitions of scarcity and deprivation); the irreducible uncertainty which prevails in international relations; and the constant temptation facing individuals to avoid the commands and sanctions of moral rules for their own advantage and to the detriment of others. Moore's analysis suggests that only the first of these causes may to some extent be removed. His contribution to that end is an analysis of the rational basis of a potentially just political order. This theme is subsequently developed in *Injustice*.

At a third and still deeper level, three contradictions are built into the text and give it an unintended ironic quality. First, in this book Moore seems to have come up with an objective measure of the moral worth of social orders, which he was unable to do in *Political Power and Social Theory*. However, his attempts to apply this calculus suggest that most of the causes of morally unacceptable social arrangements cannot actually be removed. Second, Moore opens his book with the expressed intention of discovering the potential for reducing the level of avoidable misery within societies. However, he discovers in a series of related contexts that the degree of satisfaction or discontent felt by individuals or groups is related not simply to the level of costs and benefits they experience themselves but also to the principles in terms of which these costs and benefits are distributed throughout the whole population. The focus of his argument shifts from the level of suffering experienced within a society to the principle of reciprocity underlying the distribution of benefits and costs between groups within it.

Third, despite the apparent attraction of the utilitarian moral calculus as a rational basis for the evaluation of political orders, the dismal nature of the conclusions reached by Moore on this basis lead him to insist upon the contingency of the very principles he is applying. He writes: 'rationality is and has to remain an historical conception that changes in accord with changing knowledge that can never be perfect nor complete' (1972, p.78). Having devoted the preceding three chapters to exploring ways of reducing misery, his chapter on intellectual freedom presents a competing principle – the importance of maintaining open enquiry with a view to improving rationality – whose importance seems at least equal to the utilitarian principle already espoused. Various practical compromises between institutional arrangements expressing the two principles are suggested. However, Moore does not make it clear what the logical or philosophical relationship between the two principles might be.

Two abiding impressions are left from reading *Reflections on the Causes of Human Misery*. The first is that while, on the one hand, Moore hopes that increases in the rational capacity and moral understanding of human beings will enable them to eliminate suffering and promote happiness, on the other hand he also fears that such rational and moral advances may only reveal the intrinsic impossibility of making significant advances towards these ends within any feasible form of social order. The second impression is that Moore believes that the forms of cohesion and conflict which are found within political orders derive from *moral* understandings and disagreements. The latter ultimately determine the kinds of social compromise which are acceptable to human beings in particular instances within the range of possibilities offered by any given level of technological and intellectual development. This approach is evident throughout his major works, beginning with *Soviet Politics*.

Part III

Revolution and Reciprocity

4
Politics and Power

Man has been concerned with the role of ideas in the shaping of
human behaviour ever since the first member of the species
attempted to influence the behaviour of another by exhortation
instead of blows. Throughout the centuries and in modern times
a wide variety of views have been presented on the subject . . .
Granted and even emphasizing that ideas cannot be effective
without economic (and other) changes, there is still another
important point to be made. Without strong moral feelings and
indignation, human beings will not act against the social order.
In this sense moral convictions become an equally necessary
element for changing the social order, along with alterations in
the economic structure.

The two quotations, which have been deliberately run together
above, come from the first chapter of Moore's first major work,
Soviet Politics – The Dilemma of Power (1950, p.1) and the last
chapter of his latest book, *Injustice* (1978, p.469). Even though the
composition of the latter took place almost three decades after the
former, they might easily have come from the same paragraph.
Although shifts in emphasis, tone and tactics in Moore's work
before and after *Social Origins* have been indicated in the last two
chapters of this present book, the overwhelming impression is that
Moore's writing as a whole displays an impressive degree of thematic unity.

The unity of Moore's work makes it possible to treat his first and
latest books, which focus upon the cases of Russia and Germany
respectively, as going a long way towards providing the 'missing
chapters' on those societies which, according to the writer, were
discarded from *Social Origins* (1969a, pp.viii–ix). Similarly, *Terror and Progress USSR* and the final two essays on contemporary
America in *Reflections on the Causes of Human Misery* complement *Social Origins* in two ways. First, along with *Soviet Politics*,
they provide an analysis of tendencies within Soviet Russia and the

USA *after* the decisive shift away from commercialised agrarian polity to modernising industrial state had occurred. Second, they contain attempts to assess the possibilities and costs of various patterns of future development in the USA and Russia. In the latter case at least, sufficient time has elapsed since the publication of *Terror and Progress USSR* in 1954 to enable some comments, however brief and tentative, to be made on his judgements in that book.

Perception of the unity of purpose in Moore's work may have been hindered by two of its features. First, different elements of his rather complex theoretical approach have been predominant in successive books. Second, the roles of historian, sociologist, moral arbiter and political theorist have been combined in different proportions in successive texts. In *Soviet Politics*, functionaiist considerations are very evident. Moore discusses three aspects of post-revolutionary Russia: the restrictions that the functional re-quirements of industrial society and external relations imposed upon the attempted realisation of a utopian ideology; the functions that an ambiguous ideology could perform for a totalitarian regime in an industrialising society; and the dilemmas and cost unavoid-ably imposed upon such a regime and members of the society in which it held power. These dilemmas are explored further in *Terror and Progress USSR*, a book which analyses the potential costs of various possible strategies open to the regime in the early 1950s. Two themes which emerge strongly are: the social and psychological pressures which are imposed upon individuals and groups by participation in a totalitarian society; and the conse-quences of such a society for the development of ideas of truth and beauty as manifest in the conditions of existence of Russian scien-tists and artists. In *Social Origins*, Moore's concern with the reg-ularities and costs of historical change is expressed in a scheme which has a strong evolutionary flavour. The search for the general in the particular – that is to say, for evidence of general processes as expressed in the historical events occurring in a number of societies – becomes the guiding theme. This book had been pre-ceded, as has been seen, by *Political Power and Social Theory*, in which Moore adopts the stance of the self-conscious methodolog-ist. It was followed by *Reflections on the Causes of Human Misery*, in which he appears as an equally self-conscious moral analyst. Finally, in *Injustice*, Moore emerges as a political theorist

who exploits the evidence provided by a strategically chosen historical case study to develop an approach to the analysis of political authority which is tempered by functionalist, evolutionary and
utilitarian considerations and a subtle evocation of the interplay
between society, personality and culture.

At the end of Chapter 2 it was argued that Moore had by the
1950s specified four tasks which the student of society should seek
to carry out. These were: to reconcile the study of unique events
with the search for general processes; to identify the limits and
range of choice in human affairs; to distinguish those aspects of
society which recur through time and space from those aspects
which manifest cumulative growth and change; and to specify a
workable procedure for making the moral choices which people
face within the limits imposed by history and by certain unchanging aspects of human societies. These objectives are clearly over-
lapping and, taking this into account, the following procedure will
be adopted as a means of observing the ways in which Moore has
pursued them. First, the constants of social life identified by
Moore will be examined, with particular reference to *Soviet
Politics*. Second, Moore's search for the general in the particular
will be analysed, paying special attention to *Social Origins*. This
section will include a discussion of Moore's strategy of historical
analysis. Third, the calculus of options and costs carried out by
Moore will be investigated as set out in *Terror and Progress USSR*
and his essays on 'predatory democracy'. Finally, Moore's procedures for evaluating forms of political authority and their human
consequences will be discussed with reference to *Injustice*. It
should be acknowledged immediately that this scheme will not
adequately contain or express within its rather arbitrary limits all
the subtle interconnections of Moore's multi-faceted analyses. As
a consequence these limits will continually be broken.

The dilemma of power

A glance at *Soviet Politics* tends to confirm the argument that
Moore's work as a whole displays considerable thematic unity.
Among the issues touched upon, however briefly, in the complex
but well-controlled argument of this book are the consequences of
political systems for human misery and happiness (1950, pp.38,

411), the nature of exploitation (p.411), the element of reciprocity in relations between the elite and the people (p.245), the significance of moral codes in relation to justice (p.128), the part played by conflict and frustration in the criteria for evaluating societies (p.11), the significance of intellectual criticism (p.158), and the role of legitimate opposition to political authority (p.169). These hints were to be developed more fully in later work.

In *Soviet Politics* Moore confronts two related issues. The first of these is the conflict between the proclaimed ideological goals of the Bolsheviks, with their strong emphasis upon equality, and the imperatives dictated by the means adopted to achieve, exercise and maintain power in an industrialising society in the face of severe internal and external threats. The second issue concerns the consequences for political organisation within industrial society of the need to maintain a complex division of labour associated with inequalities of power and rewards. Moore examines the response of the Bolshevik leadership to these problems in three phases. First, he studies the tactics which were adopted to capture and secure control of the Russian state. Subsequently he explores the dilemmas faced in the exercise of political authority during the period culminating in Stalin's establishment as effective dictator. Finally, he deals with the period of Stalinist rule until 1950. With respect to each phase Moore concentrates upon three related issues. These are: the dilemmas imposed upon party leaders by the constraints of ideology, functional imperatives and international relations; the costs and benefits of the attempted solutions adopted in response to these dilemmas; and the further structural problems which the attempted solutions brought into being.

In the early chapters of *Soviet Politics* Moore explores the ways in which Bolshevik ideology entered into and interacted with the practical considerations involved in making and defending a revolution in a particular agrarian society. He shows that the initial predictions of Lenin with respect to the development of Russia and her capitalist neighbours were contradicted by, first, the failure of the quasi-bourgeois republican government which took power early in 1917 to end the war with Germany and undertake significant social reform, and, second, the absence of successful proletarian revolutions in other 'imperialist' European societies. The response to the former failure was Lenin's call in 1917 for a republic of soviets as a proletarian organisation which would combat bourgeois influence. The absence of other successful revolutions in neighbouring societies was one of the circumstances which contributed to the eventual establishment of Stalinism.

Moore makes a distinction between the Bolshevik 'ideology of ends' which envisaged 'the creation of a state in which eventually every cook could govern' (p.42) and the 'ideology of means' which specified the organisational techniques by which the party would capture and retain power. Secrecy and elitism within the party in combination with the discipline necessary to successful conspirators were important components of the ideology of means. These were the realities that lay behind the strategy of 'democratic centralism'. Once in power the application of judicious terror combined with persuasion and example would, it was claimed, create support and understanding among the masses, who were, as yet, not to be trusted. Moore notes: 'While the ideology of ends has been much modified or discarded, the ideology of means has had lasting importance' (p.60).

The role of the Marxist-Leninist tradition of ideas in Soviet Russia, argues Moore, has been to identify the important questions relevant to the ideology of means and to provide acceptable ways of asking them. Above all, these have been questions about power: Who holds it? How do economic and other developments affect its distribution? How may these factors be manipulated to favour communist interests? (p.115). Against this background, ideologically acceptable ways had to be found to solve the following problems which are intrinsic to *all* political regimes in industrialising societies. First, how is industry to be organised? For example, how are the factors or production (people, capital, materials) to be combined, production goals specified and products distributed? Second, how is labour discipline to be maintained? For example, how are the workers to be organised and internally differentiated? What part are trade unions to play? Third, how are the city and the countryside to be made to work together so that the peasantry support by their food production and political acquiescence (or, at least, quiescence) the social order of the cities? Fourth, what system of status, authority and discipline should be established within the ruling groups and within the society at large? Finally, what relationships should be maintained with the rest of the world? (pp.85–7).

The part played by ideology in confronting these problems

becomes clear when the outcome of the New Economic Policy (NEP) introduced in 1921 is considered. The government had retained control over the 'commanding heights' of the economy but permitted private enterprise to flourish in many areas of industry and agriculture: 'If a group of Manchester Liberals had been in control of Russia at this time, they would not have perceived any dilemma' (p.95). However, the forces making for economic recovery were either actively or passively opposed to the regime of the Bolsheviks. While members of the government agreed on the need to maintain the party's monopoly of power and eventually to undertake a socialist transformation of Russian society, they disagreed about the relationship between these objectives and the means by which they might be attained. Moore compares the alternative strategies of Trotsky and Bukharin. The former wanted to push ahead quickly towards socialist transformation at home and abroad while the latter proposed a cautious extension of cooperation between the industrial and agricultural sectors within the framework of the NEP. Moore argues that the solutions implemented by Stalin, which combined elements of both the above strategies as well as his own distinctive contribution, were equally an attempt to reconcile the imperatives of survival with the achievement of the ideological goals specified above. The tensions in Russian society generated by the NEP meant that the solution was bound to be an authoritarian one.

Moore traces the implementation of this authoritarian policy during the 1920s and early 1930s. Its main features were: the exploitation of democratic sentiments as a means of directing popular hostility towards minor officials and away from the party hierarchy; the elimination of organised opposition in the name of 'the dictatorship of the proletariat'; the reduction of the soviets to the role of local administrative agencies for the party leadership; the development of bureaucratic means, such as the secret police and 'control commissions', to monitor central and local administration and maximise the information available to the elite; and the promotion of a mythology of proletarian control which justified the castration of the trade unions (since class struggle had officially been done away with) and permitted the introduction of income differentials within the labour force.   The largest section of *Soviet Politics* is devoted to an exploration of the inconsistencies and dilemmas which were embodied in the structure of the Stalinist regime during the late 1930s and 1940s. By the mid-1930s the reigning ideology was beginning 'to approach more closely the actual facts of the distribution of power in the Russian state', while still retaining and exploiting the democratic and populist aspects of communism. An outstanding characteristic of these years was, argues Moore, 'the endeavour to reconcile the older Leninist doctrine that the masses are the masters of the country with the fact of the concentration of power at the top levels of the Party. Lenin's theory of a conspiratorial and disciplined elite provided a basic starting point in this process' (pp.221–2). The increased coincidence of ideology and political reality was expressed in, for example, the formal recognition of the Party's leading role within the Russian state in article 126 of the 1936 Constitution, and the insistence that the freedom of the individual depended upon the particular framework of socio-political organisation that the Soviet state happened to enshrine (article 125).

However, this framework was riddled with contradictions. For example, the official abolition of class conflict did not entail the abolition of classes, the latter feature being a consequence of the functional importance of status inequalities in an industrial society, argues Moore. He suggests that Soviet Russia and the USA are similar in that respect at least (pp.238–43, 246). A further conflict of principle existed between the authoritarian organisation of the society and the persistence of 'a genuine residue . . . of democracy at the lower levels of the Party' (p.276). More fundamental, perhaps, was the contradiction between the vested interest of a totalitarian ruler in confusion and uncertainty within the bureaucracy and the vested interest of his subordinates in predictability. A complex system of bureaucratic monitoring had the effect of breaking up 'protective alliances' at the lower levels. They could not be exploited as a means of co-ordinating effort because of the danger of their forming a basis for political opposition (pp.295–7).

Moore argues that the regulation of the Soviet industrial order has taken place through a contradictory mixture of bureaucratic controls and market mechanisms such as competition and the profit motive. The instrusion of the market has not been permitted in the sphere of labour supply, where it would have increased the power of the trade unions. In respect of the peasantry a large-scale frontal attack was made through the collectivisation of agriculture upon a way of life in which the market had a significant role. Even here, however, the continued dependence of the economy upon peasant production on private plots was evident. In practice, the regime has emphasised the maintenance of party control within society and central control within the Party, 'borrowing just enough from the capitalist competitors to make their own system function' (p.316). This borrowing was one aspect of the regime's attempt to wrestle with yet another fundamental contradiction. This consists in the fact that like American culture Soviet culture is materialistic. It exacts effort and obedience from its population in return for the promise of improved material conditions. In Moore's words, 'on the one hand the system emphasises the desirability of material goods; on the other hand, it is unable to satisfy this demand' (p.316).

Finally, in the course of three chapters on the foreign policy of the Soviet regime, Moore argues that although the expectation of revolutions abroad had an important impact upon this policy in the early years of the Soviet state, the Russian leaders were 'forced to fall back on the techniques of traditional balance-of-power diplomacy' (p.215). Before the Second World War their major problem was the difficulty of splitting the capitalist front while engaging in a policy of encouraging communism abroad that tended to unite their enemies. However, this dilemma was ultimately secondary to the fact that the 'structure of international relationships itself imposes certain types of behaviour upon the participants' (p.351). The intrinsic dynamics of coalition and counter-coalition were influenced by the suspicions and preconceptions deriving from the ideologies of partners and opponents. However, in the final analysis, 'The choice of antagonists or allies has been determined not primarily by ideological factors, but by the structure of the balance-of-power system itself' (p.383). These chapters contain a detailed and persuasive analysis of the interaction between foreign relations and the processes of communist takeover in Eastern Europe and China. Moore does not minimise the complexity of these issues, emphasising that the 'connection between the internal organization of a society and its foreign policy is a complex question that cannot yet be answered on the basis of simple formulas' (p.396).

In *Soviet Politics*, through a remarkable synthesis of historical, sociological and psychological perspectives, Moore provides an explanation of the development of Soviet Russia up until 1950.

The achievement of his analysis is to have identified the intrinsic requirements that had to be satisfied and the intrinsic limits upon the ambitions which could be realised in that society at that time. These limits and requirements derived in part from the need to manage an industrial society and maintain the security of a political regime within a given social structure and international setting. They also derived from the constraints of an ideology that, while satisfying the 'apparent necessity' for a set of beliefs which were 'in part above and beyond rational criticism' (p.409), imposed yet further demands which restricted the leadership's freedom of manoeuvre.[1] While stressing the inconsistencies between different goals embodied in the ideology of means and the ideology of ends, Moore also notices that a great deal of practical compromise is possible, especially if emotional commitment to established symbols may continue to be satisfied in the context of subtly transformed practices. Moore is sensitive not only to the different levels of awareness manifest in ideological belief and the possibility that contradictory beliefs might be psychologically compatible but also to the rigidities and preconceptions built into the structure of language itself (pp.276, 413–17). By the concluding chapter Moore is entering into vigorous and sympathetic debate with writers such as W. G. Sumner, Sebastian De Grazia and A. L. Kroebner. He is beginning to explore in more general terms some of the affinities and conflicts contained in the relations between patterns of human perception and practice, the constraints and potentialities of cultural symbols, the functional requirements of social life and the political purposes of rulers.

Lord and peasant

It was argued in Chapter 3 that Moore's theoretical position at the time when he began writing *Social Origins* could be understood as expressing a balance between the desire for intellectual order, fidelity to the facts and a determination to keep the door to moral choice wedged firmly open. Moore's practical application of this strategy is related to his implementation of three related intellectual techniques: discovery, explanation and moral assessment.

Moral assessment entails a judgement of the consequences of an event or structural change. Its basis is a calculation, drawing upon all the factual evidence available, of the costs and benefits in terms of human suffering or freedom caused or avoided by that event or structural change. The calculation includes those costs or benefits potentially due to alternative events or structural changes which might have happened but did not.

By discovery is meant the intellectual apprehension of con- straining facts that exist independently of the observer's being or desires. Among these discoverable facts are the perceptions and moral values of individuals and groups and also the characteristics of social relationships, including the intrinsic limitations upon their potential for adaptation and change without disintegration. Some of these discoverable facts may be found to be present in practi- cally all known societies; others may be found only in societies at a particular stage in the evolution of technological, organisational and intellectual forms; still others may be found to be peculiar to specific societies or historical periods or even to particular groups or individuals. Discovery of these facts and their disposition in time and space occurs through the collection and rational analysis of evidence. An important limitation is that one cannot predict the future existence of particular facts. Nevertheless it is possible to predict, with respect to those alternative events or structural changes that are known to be possible, their likely consequences for social relationships and perceptions whose potential for trans- formation at a given stage of social evolution has been discovered. However, such a calculation is subject to two difficulties: the unpredictability of the consequences of future facts peculiar to specific societies, groups or individuals; and the unpredictability of possible innovations in intellectual, organisation and technological capacities which would constitute the arrival of a new stage in social evolution.

Moore assumes the existence of a dialectical relationship between discovery and moral assessment. The locations in time and space which the researcher chooses to investigate in his or her search for relevant data are determined by a preliminary judge- ment about the events and structural changes which probably had, in the past, or are likely to have, in the future, morally significant consequences in terms of human suffering or freedom. The facts which are subsequently discovered provide the basis for moral assessment. It should be noted that within the limits indicated above the same procedures are employed for moral assessment of possible events and structural changes in the future as are used for assessing the past, taking into account the possibility of suppressed historical alternatives. This is an important point because the same cannot be said of Moore's procedure for arriving at historical *explanations* or events and structural changes. The logical structure of Moore's procedure for assessing the consequences of past occurrences is the same as his procedure for assessing the likely consequences of possible future occurrences. However, he does not propose that the procedures appropriate for arriving at an explanation of past occurrences can be used to predict future occurrences.

Moore is concerned with three kinds of change. First, there are cyclical changes such as the alternation between feudalism, rational bureaucracy and totalitarianism which Moore sees as 'recurring subpatterns' found in a wide range of complex societies at differing levels of development (1958, p.29). Change of this kind is a consequence of the intrinsic structural contradictions characteristic of the finite range of organisational forms which may be employed to co-ordinate the behaviour of large numbers of human beings. Second, there are the changes associated with the gradually increasing level of exploitation of the potential for resource appropriation and the exercise of power made possible by successive stages of social evolution. These changes appear as long-term transformations involving many societies in the ways in which social groups organise their relationships with one another. Examples include the implementation of more systematic taxation methods due to advances in military technology and bureaucratic techniques or the steady extension of the cash nexus accompanied by the growth of the urban market.

An explanation of both the transition between stages of social evolution and the gradual realisation of the transforming potential within each stage seems to reside in the competitive advantages to individuals, groups and societies which the new techniques present. This, of course, does not explain variations in the rate or degree of change in particular cases. Moore's notion of modernisation as used in *Social Origins* seems to refer to this kind of change. He appears to mean by it the processes whereby, through the implementation of technological, organisational and intellectual innovations the degree of surplus extracted from the labouring population is increased and its appropriation managed in ways which improve the capacity of newly emerging or established elites, including the managers of the state apparatus, to advance or seek to maintain their relative power both within their own society and in relation to elites in other societies. Major outcomes of these processes in particular societies are the development of industry and a strong centralised government (1969a, pp.270, 385–6, 441–2, 467–8).

The third kind of change refers to events which are the occasion of rapid structural transformations in particular societies whose consequences are relevant to Moore's moral concerns. Such events might, for example, take the form of civil wars or revolutions. Although an interest in understanding morally significant changes stimulates the search for a historical explanation of these changes, Moore insists that there is no logical relationship between the process of assessing moral consequences and the process of discovering causes. Explanation is, as has just been implied, regarded by Moore as a process of discovery which never reaches completion because of the inaccessibility of a proportion of the relevant facts. In terms of the approach adopted in *Social Origins* an adequate explanation of a particular structural change in a specific society would include answers to the following questions:

1. What were the potentialities for and limits upon structural variation in a society at that stage of social development, given the functional requirements that had to be met for it to continue in existence and the intrinsic characteristics of the organisational, technological and intellectual techniques available to carry them out? This question might be answered through a mixture of comparative analysis and 'imaginary experiment' (e.g. 1969a, pp.40, 114–15, 125–6).
2. What tendencies towards cohesion and distintegration were actually present in the social configuration through which the division of the labour and the co-ordination of social life were carried out? (e.g. pp.132–4, 140, 162–74, 208–27)
3. What perceptions did members of this society located at different points within this social configuration have of their material and moral interests? (e.g. pp.17, 55–6, 65–9, 181, 235–6, 334–41, 484–7)
4. What specific events occurred which presented a threat to these perceived material and moral interests sufficiently sud-

den and/or drastic to stimulate them into action? (e.g. pp.136–41, 251)

5. In what ways did their perceptions of their moral and material interests and of this threat lead them to distinguish between potential allies and potential opponents or victims? (e.g. pp.18, 92–101, 121–3, 128–9)

6. What options in historical development had been closed off as a result of preceding sequences of structural change? (e.g. pp.140–1, 151–3, 251–4)

7. In what ways did people actually behave after the threat had occurred and how is their behaviour to be interpreted in terms of the answers to (3), (4) and (5) above? (e.g. pp.70–92, 353–70)

8. What were the outcomes of their behaviour in terms of structural change, whether or not such change was intended by them, and how are these changes to be accounted for in terms of the answers to (1), (2) and (6) above? (e.g. pp.18–20, 108–10, 149–55)

Two points arising from the above may now be discussed. First, an important feature of this strategy of explanation is that it is not sufficient simply to identify the relevant society as an example of one of a limited range of types of society possible at a given stage of social evolution, e.g. feudal polity, caste society, centralised bureaucracy. Explanation also requires detailed knowledge about particular groups and even individuals in the society at points in time immediately before the events embodying the structural change took place. Second, a major part is played by identifiable social groups and individuals making moral and material choices. Although the structural outcomes of their choices are a product of the interplay between human action and the discoverable constraints and opportunities characterising a given society at a particular stage of evolution and with a particular historical past, these structural outcomes cannot be explained solely with reference to these constraints and opportunities. The choices that human beings make have to be recognised. Once these choices have been made, their rationality may be explained with reference to knowledge about the perceptions of the people making the choices. However, recognition of the part played by these choices entails recognition that other choices were possible. This introduces an important element of indeterminacy. Thus, for example, while it may be argued that some of the structural consequences of the French Revolution were necessary in order to produce the desired outcome of 'democracy' and that this event was 'crucial' it is not possible to say that the Revolution was 'inevitable' (p.108). Through this strategy of explanation Moore combines elements of functionalism, evolutionary theory and a recognition of the part played by human beings making choices influenced by perceptions, moral dilemmas and material interests grounded in specific forms of life.

The same strategy of explanation is employed by Moore with reference to structural changes which were less rapid and dramatic, though arguably as costly in terms of violence and repression over a longer period. Such changes include the adoption of particular forms of commercialised agriculture by members of the landed aristocracy in some of the societies with which he deals. In both types of case the threat faced by social groups, who are habitually identified in class terms with reference to the societal division of labour, stemmed from the competitive processes within or between societies intrinsic to modernisation. Having discussed Moore's procedures of moral assessment and explanation in *Social Origins* and their relationship to the discovery of facts, the way in which he incorporates these techniques in his overall analysis will now be considered.

Causes and consequences

The basic model employed by Moore, in terms of which he locates his comparative analyses, is of a differentiated, hierarchical and to some degree repressive social order integrated through a combination of familistic, quasi-familistic, bureaucratic, commercial and other bonds. Moore employs the conventional distinction between a society organised around ascriptive principles of distribution, i.e. one based upon inherited social status, and a society organised around achievement, i.e. one based upon a system of rewarding individual performance, for example through the market or within a bureaucracy. This implicit assumption is made explicit in *Injustice* (p.451). While the latter of these 'polar types' is 'inherently unstable', the former assumes 'a static society existing in a static environment'.[2]

Moore's analyses of agrarian societies indicate the presence of the cash nexus and bureaucratic tendencies at very early stages of their development. The extension of both types of social relationship increases the significance of state officials and merchants as opposed to the great landowners. However, Moore does not assume that the functional or class location of a social group by itself determines the content of its members' values with respect to the practices of bureaucracy and commerce. He cites examples of 'feudalized' bourgeoisies (e.g. in France), commercially minded aristocracies (e.g. in England) as well as bureaucrats with strong familistic leanings (e.g. in China) or a disposition towards the diffuse ties of feudalism (e.g. in Japan). Nor does Moore assume that any one kind of resource or capacity, such as physical force, rule-making power or property ownership, is especially determining.

Within the model described above Moore focuses upon changes in the forms of asymmetrical and conflictual interdependence which bind together peasants, landlords, manipulators of the cash nexus and the managers of royal or public bureaucracies. He introduces us to the challenges presented by the processes of modernisation to specific groups of men and women accustomed to particular established forms of life. These forms of life, such as the medieval English village, the Southern plantation, the *daimyō* estate in Tokugawa Japan, and so on, were located within broader societal configurations expressing interdependencies shaped by the division of labour and the appropriation of the surplus.

The 'active ingredient' common to all Moore's cases was a marked increase in the rate of change in the direction of a more bureaucratised and/or commercialised society, a fairly rapid advance which placed established material and moral interest under threat. Of particular interest to Moore are the reactions of landlords and peasants since their involvement in the established rural structures was greatest. The forms taken by the threat varied. Bureaucratisation and commercialisation did not always occur at the same pace as each other (1969a, pp.467–8), and the pressures they exerted were sometimes closely associated with the intrusive influence of other societies. This was so in the cases of China (pp.175–7), Japan (pp.234, 241, 251), India (pp.341, 352) and Germany (p.440). Moore is concerned with two modalities of the rural order's response to commercialisation and bureaucratisation: its confrontation and accommodation with modernising urban society; and the transformation of forms of domination in the countryside. In respect of both Moore is concerned with the costs of particular sequences of modernisation and their implications for the dialectic between repression and freedom.

Moore's argument in *Social Origins* was described in some detail in Chapter 1 but some salient points will be very briefly reviewed. Broadly speaking, the response of the great landowners to the threats associated with modernisation either strengthened their interdependence with the managers of the state apparatus or led them into closer association with the urban bourgeoisie. In the case of France both responses occurred, binding all three interests into a quarrelsome triangle. In the English case, however, aristocrats and merchants found common cause against the crown. A further variation with strong authoritarian tendencies was the use of the combined might of the landed interest and the state, as in Japan and Germany, to keep the bourgeoisie politically weak. Where political weakness on the part of the latter coincided with entrepreneurial feebleness, as in Russia and China, the resulting elite coalition was able neither to inhibit the growth nor to contain the eventual impact of massively disruptive pressures stemming from the peasantry. The potential for such pressures to become a threat to the existing social order was in part a consequence of the way relations between the great landowners and their rural labour force had developed.

In cases where the degree of reciprocity between lord and peasant was weak, where the structure of the peasant village was conducive to organised revolt and the repressive capacity of the local and central powers at a low level, then peasant revolution was a possibility. In the case of Russia all three conditions were satisfied at the time of the Revolution. The work of the Red Army in China helped to bring the second and third conditions into existence and thus make revolution possible there also. In India the revolutionary potential has been inhibited by the caste system. The possibility of revolution was taken off the agenda in Japan by, *inter alia*, the maintenance of a high degree of solidarity between rural social classes, in Germany by the application of an effective system of repressive labour control, in England by the destruction of peasant society, and in the USA by the absence of a peasantry.

In Moore's view, democracy has developed in societies where the employment of violence and repression has been largely restricted to eliminating or subordinating rural interests hostile to forms of commercial growth adapted to a free labour market. As the social class most benefiting from the free labour market, the bourgeoisie has been able to establish a powerful position in the social order which is, however, short of monopolistic domination. Democratic values express the importance of shared responsibility for making political rules which include the reliable provision of protection for individual freedom. By contrast fascism has developed in societies where repression has been used, increasingly through the agency of the state, to raise the level of rural surplus appropriation, maintain the material advantages of the landed interest and incorporate the bourgeoisie and industrial workforce within an authoritarian polity. Fascist values may be understood as an inversion of democratic values, in Moore's view. Communist regimes have developed in societies where repression and violence have been used, first, to eliminate the landed aristocracy through peasant revolution, and, second, to transform the peasantry through the agency of a revolutionary elite, in the absence of a significant bourgeoisie. Communist values entail the pursuit of a supposedly 'higher' freedom than that made possible by democracy.

Moore is concerned with two kinds of process in *Social Origins*. One kind of process is relevant to his discussion of causal explanations; the other is derived from his moral assessment of consequences. For convenience I shall label the first as 'causal processes' and the latter as 'consequential processes'. Examples of causal processes are the extension of bureaucracy and commerce. Through a procedure which was analysed above Moore seeks to demonstrate that these processes presented threats to members of particular social classes in specific societies, and that their responses, constrained or facilitated by specific attributes of the social structure, resulted in a variety of structural changes. It is noticeable that Moore pays particular attention to the elements of violence and repression involved in such changes. This leads on to the second kind of process which concerns the sequence of *conse-*

quences flowing from the responses of social groups, including the urban bourgeoisie and state officials, to the dilemmas of modernisation. Moore's moral concern with the costs and benefits of modernisation leads him to concentrate selectively upon that subset of consequences which have a discoverable relationship to desired or abhorred outcomes, respectively democracy and dictatorship. He categorises consequences in terms of their morally relevant effects, in other words their tendency to increase suffering and/or to bring about the establishment of democratic freedoms. The process which occurs through the sequence of consequences is the interplay between suffering and the reduction or increase of freedom. The facts which are relevant include evidence about the suffering caused by what actually happened and evidence, in so far as it is available, about what would have happened if other consequences had been produced.

One way to distinguish between causal processes and consequential processes is to note that processes of bureaucratisation have a *similar* structure in different societies, though, in interaction with other processes of the same kind, such as commercialisation, they may have a wide range of structural consequences. By contrast, the processes whereby freedom is increased culminating in democracy are likely to exhibit considerable structural *variation* between societies, though their culmination is similar in those societies. Two other points may be added. First, both causal processes and consequential processes traverse political boundaries. Commercial and bureaucratic pressures stemming from one society can have a profound impact in another; the examples of China and India cited by Moore come to mind. Similarly, the movement towards democratic freedom may advance through the development of institutional arrangements which incorporate this characteristic to progressively higher degrees in different societies in successive historical periods (p.427). Second, just as bureaucratisation and commercialisation may be of either similar or unequal strength in the same society, so processes leading to democracy and dictatorship may compete for priority in the same society. These competing tendencies may be affected by decisive human choices between historical alternatives, as in early nineteenth-century England (1969a, pp.31–2; 1978, p.474). They may also produce a kind of mutual inhibition, as in France, where, in Moore's opinion, the peasantry both made the Revolution possible and prevented its full democratic potential from being realised.

Tradition and style

Before making some critical comments on Moore's analysis I want to notice four aspects of his presentation. First, Moore hardly ever misses an opportunity to oppose attempts to reduce the analytical significance of structural constraints, particularly those rooted in property and political power. He is merciless in his scorn for explanations which reduce these constraints to statistical series (e.g. pp.15, 36–7, 46, 52, 67, 165), cultural factors (e.g. pp.49, 58, 62) or psychology (e.g. pp.52, 113, 178, 335). Moore does not neglect any of these aspects of explanation on principle, as his other work shows; nor is he blind to the importance of 'ways of seeing'. Indeed his capacity to persuade the reader that he is introducing the latter to the perceptions of those groups whose dilemmas are being described is impressive. However, perceptions always have to be explained somehow, and structural factors tend to carry more weight in the argument of *Social Origins* than psychological theories or cultural generalisations. To cite just one example, the issues which 'could or could not come to the surface' before the American Civil War were to a great extent determined by the 'alignment of the main social groupings' rather than, say, psychological dispositions or cultural leanings (p.132).

Second, Moore tends to conduct his historical case studies through a kind of self-interrogation. This directs him to his data in a search during which the reader is treated as an active partner, privy to Moore's musings and doubts. His chapters tend to begin with questions or puzzles in their early paragraphs: 'Why did the process of industrialization in England culminate in the establishment of a relatively free society?' (p.4); 'How and why there was any similarity at all in the final political outcome [between France and England] during the nineteenth and twentieth centuries constitutes, along with the important differences, the central puzzle that I shall try to unravel in this chapter' (p.40); 'Why did [the American Civil War] happen? Why did our vaunted capacity for settling our differences fail us at this point?' (p.113); 'How were the upper classes [in China] connected with the land in this society where the overwhelming majority were tillers of the soil?' (p.162);

'What explains the difference between the course of modernization in Japan and that in both Russia and China?' (p.229) The
questions occur throughout (e.g. pp.56, 104, 115, 149, 204, 208,
245, 252). Perhaps significantly, the one case study where this
technique is absent is the chapter on India, to which I shall shortly
return. The ubiquitous question-mark and the first person singular
are distinctive marks of Moore's style. The general effect is to
persuade the reader that he or she is sifting the evidence along
with Moore and, like him, is surveying the points for and against
competing explanations. Cast in the role of Dr Watson, the reader
is flattered when Moore, who does not employ the 'royal' we,
confidentially murmurs 'The main point for our purposes . . .'
(p.184).[3]

This style of presentation is allied to a strategy of constant
scanning for comparisons over time and space. Much of the book's
power flows from the minute plotting of similarities and differences *within* the particular case studies that complements the
broad comparative analysis which culminates in the final part. This
process of skilful cross-reference operates as a kind of radar identifying the longitude and latitude of the argument every few pages.[4]

A further feature of the text, which gives it moral as well as
intellectual 'bite', is the almost rhythmical resurgence of the demand that we remember the victims of social change. Like Scrooge
on Christmas Eve, we are forced to see the ghosts of Christmas
Past and Christmas Present. We are reminded of the losers who
suffered from the enclosures (p.12), who did the dirty work in the
English Revolution (p.16), who experienced the rod of the *ancien
régime* and the sword of revolutionary 'terror' (pp.103–4), and so
on. In this respect *Social Origins* might be regarded as being,
perhaps not intentionally, both a compliment and a corrective to
the work of Adam Smith. Moore accepts, in the spirit of Smith,
that the freedoms of modern Western democracy, that is to say

> the right to vote, representation in a legislature which makes
> the laws and hence is more than a rubber stamp for the execu-
> tive, an objective system of law that at least in theory confers no
> special privileges on account of birth or inherited status, secur-
> ity for the rights of property and the elimination of barriers
> inherited from the past on its use, religious toleration, freedom
> of speech and the right to peaceful assembly

were 'Worked out in connection with the rise of modern capitalism' (p.429). He also believes, like Smith, that not only the implementation of wrong-headed doctrine (e.g. mercantilism, fascism) but also the rational pursuit of happiness by an individual was likely to promote misery among his or her fellows to some degree (Gay, 1969, pp.359–68).

Adam Smith recognised the importance of the economic relations between rural producers and the city, declaring in *The Wealth of Nations* that 'The great commerce of every civilized society is that carried on between the inhabitants of the town and those of the country' (1976, p.376). Smith was particularly concerned with the supposedly beneficial effects of commerce and industry upon rural ways:

> Commerce and manufactures gradually introduced order and good government, and with them, the liberty and security of individuals, among the inhabitants of the country, who had before lived in a continual state of war with their neighbours, and of servile dependency upon their superiors. This, though it has been the least observed, is by far the most important of their effects. (Smith, 1976, p.412)

Moore's analysis counterbalances this urbanite view of the world by pointing out not only the threatening aspects of commerce (and its frequent companion, bureaucracy) when seen from the peasant village or the chateau but also the reflex action of rural social classes upon the city and the state.[5]

It is not my intention to present *Social Origins* as the product of some imaginary and ethereal debate in the clouds between Adam Smith, Montesquieu, Bentham, Hegel and Barrington Moore. However, the works of the writers mentioned have become incorporated within the body of intellectual criticism which constitutes the more self-conscious and reflexive mode of the philosophical tradition in which Moore participates. Moore's formulation of his questions in *Social Origins*, which are broadly speaking to do with the conditions under which freedom and justice are possible and the costs of either achieving these benefits or failing to achieve them, are rooted in habits of thinking and evaluation which have developed in the West since at least the Enlightenment.

The reality of the effects of these ways of thinking in their less reflexive and less self-conscious modes is suggested by the participation of American citizens in the Second World War. Certain aspects of *Social Origins* become more understandable if that global conflict is recognised as the great and almost unmentioned event which provides the book with its shape and moral dynamism. During that war Americans were called upon to make sacrifices and in many cases to die for 'democracy' in a mortal conflict with 'dictatorship'. They were not being asked to risk their lives in the name of 'capitalism' or a 'market-oriented society' against a 'bureaucratic society with authoritarian tendencies'; nor were they being exhorted to fight across the lines of any one of the plethora of abstract typologies drawn up by sociologists or political scientists.

The terms 'dictatorship' and 'democracy' insist upon the moral differences between forms of political authority which were, respectively, 'unacceptable' and 'acceptable' to participants in a global conflict which radically altered the structure of world society. It is fundamental to Moore's analysis that the distinction between the two terms expresses a real moral difference. Furthermore, perhaps it should not be surprising that a man who served as political analyst in the Office of Strategic Studies during the Second World War should identify as crucial the differences between Britain, France and the USA (the Allies), Germany and Japan (the 'fascist' powers) and Russia and China (the partners of the democratic allies during the war). Both the Chinese Revolution and the liberation of India from colonial rule, major events in his book, were greatly influenced by the outcome of this war and occurred very soon after its conclusion.[6]

Strengths and weaknesses

It has to be acknowledged that there is a fundamental unevenness in *Social Origins* which is most evident in his treatment of the three 'democratic' cases. On the one hand, Moore's historical explanations of the causes of structurally significant outcomes such as the French Revolution, which were produced in large part by the responses of rural social classes to the threats imposed by modernisation, have considerable force. They combine the historian's relentless pursuit of specific detail with the sociologist's sensitivity to the points of rigidity and flexibility in social arrangements. On the other hand, Moore's analyses of the morally relevant conse-quences of changes are much less satisfactory. Instead of a formal analysis of the moral criteria which underly his assessments there are implicit references to the English case as being, in Moore's eyes, the nearest approach to the ideal of liberal democracy. Communism and fascism are judged, morally, in terms of the failure to achieve liberal democracy which their inauguration in any society implies.

If Moore's negative definitions of communism and fascism as moral outcomes (with their relatively unanalysed referent) are accepted as valid, then there is little difficulty in accepting the plausibility of the logical connections made by Moore between causal processes and consequential processes in the relevant cases. Readers are asked to recognise connections between events and structural changes which took place in Japan and China over relatively short periods of less than a century. Aristocratic and peasant responses to commercialisation and bureaucratisation led by fairly short historical jumps to fascist takeovers or communist regimes. Similar comments apply to Moore's much more sketchy analyses of Russia and Germany. However, when considering the consequential processes which culminated in democracy in the three 'western' cases we are asked to acknowledge the occurrence of a single process, '*the* bourgeois-democratic revolution' (p.427), which took different forms in three societies over a time period which covers over 500 years and which is identified by moral criteria which are never formally defined. When this is combined, as will be seen, with a refusal to look systematically at relations between societies, not least among the three societies concerned, a certain degree of intellectual resistance inevitably builds up.

The weaknesses that may be found in *Social Origins* stem from Moore's failure at key points to implement strategies of analysis which his theoretical position was perfectly well able to encompass but which would have damaged the moral force of the implicit references which are made throughout the book to the English case. The two analytical strategies which he neglects to pursue sufficiently are, first, investigation of the interplay between pro-cesses occurring within societies and processes occurring between societies, and second, analysis of the relatively autonomous con-straining and facilitating effects of ideologies whose appearance in particular places at particular times is as subject to historical contingency as is progress towards their realisation in institutional arrangements. The previous examination of *Soviet Politics* clearly demonstrates Moore's skill in applying both forms of analysis. Indeed, in a later essay he was to argue that to treat the USA as 'an isolated social unit' might be 'a necessity for orderly exposition but a crude violation of reality' (1972, p.164).

To have paid more attention to inter-societal relations in *Social Origins* would have had two consequences. It would have made clear that the violence of the seventeenth and eighteenth centuries in England was *not* the prelude to a 'peaceful transition' to parliamentary democracy in the nineteenth century because the violence and repression of colonial expansion in Asia and Africa and the impact of English domination over other inhabitants of the British Isles would have had to be taken into account. These were costs imposed by the English although borne by other people. It is noticeable that this part of the work concerns England rather than Britain or the British Empire. The second consequence would have been to expose the decisive effect that foreign conquest might have on the political arrangements of a society. In his preface Moore recognises that small societies are subject to the consequences of economic and political pressures stemming from large societies but he neglects to give much attention to the influence that large societies might have upon each other (p.x).

To what extent, for example, is parliamentary democracy in modern France a consequence of American victory in the Second World War? If Germany had been undefeated, would a consequent flowering of the fascist tendencies evident in pre-war and Vichy France have been explained by Moore with reference to the French Revolution? Would this event perhaps appear in a new guise? After all, like the Meiji Restoration in Japan, the French Revolution imposed a more centralised modern state apparatus and removed the legal privileges of the aristocracy while increasing the political weight of the more prosperous and commercially minded peasantry. Indeed, has not Moore already noted a resemblance between the late-nineteenth-century Japanese squire and 'the commercialising nobleman of eighteenth-century Toulouse' (p.286). It is all too easy to see how the argument might go[7].

One response to the above criticism might be to point out that the ideological content of the French Revolution was in important ways different from that of the Meiji Restoration. Moore is well aware of the shaping power of ideology upon action and devotes an appendix to 'reactionary and revolutionary imagery'. However, the gaping hiatus is a discussion of democratic imagery or ideology, its sources and transmission. Moore notes that a culture 'screens out certain parts of the objective situation and emphasises other parts' (p.485). This procedure, it may be noticed, also described the way in which Moore deliberately and as a self-conscious methodology concentrates upon a specific subset of morally significant consequences in his search for processes culminating in liberal democracy.

The content and transmission of cultures, Moore argues, have to be explained in terms of the past and present experiences of human beings in social relationships. The one suggestion he makes in regard to liberal democratic ideology is that landed aristocrats, confronted with the exactions of royal bureaucracy and the incipient influence of specialised technicians, have developed an ideal of the cultured amateur whose social authority is justified by his competence to assess the social and political implications of broad issues arising in all areas of knowledge (pp.488–9). This is a nice point and has an apparent bearing on the English case in particular. However, it is to ignore the broad stream in favour of a minor eddy. Moore pays very little attention to the part played by professionals and intellectuals (using both terms fairly loosely) whose sphere of influence resided in their function of *mediating* relations between individuals and groups, for example through the law, the church, educational institutions and, not least, parliamentary organisations. The scope for such people, their room for manoeuvre and their tendency to develop self-consciousness as a distinct group, tended to increase in societies undergoing the kind of radical social change which Moore associates with the shift between stages of social evolution.[8]

The need for such social mediators was especially great when established and new economic and political interests were gradually coming to terms with one another, no one interest having the capacity to sweep the others away or escape from partial dependence upon them. In his analysis of just such a situation in America before the Civil War, Moore is quite aware of the strategic influence possessed by politicians, journalists and clergymen, people whose work it was to 'provide the arguments, good and bad alike, both for changing the structure of society and for maintaining things as they are' (p.137). Eighteenth-century Europe provided many instances of such situations of dynamic equilibrium. Peter Gay (1966) has described the 'climate of criticism' which developed at that time. More recently, Gianfranco Poggi, drawing on the work of Habermas, has clearly set out the argument that, in this period, intellectual, literary and artistic pursuits were the focus of the developing idea of a 'public realm' within which the actions of the state and other aspects of 'public affairs' could be monitored and criticised. While not attacking the sovereignty of the state power, the 'bourgeoisie-as-public' developed a body of opinion critical of ascriptively based privilege and favourable to reforms which would institutionalise the operation of public criticism upon the actions of the state (Poggi, 1978, pp.81–4).

One of the major omissions of Moore's analysis is the failure to recognise the significance of the American Revolution in locating people holding such ideas in positions of great influence within the developing American state. Moore is perfectly prepared to acknowledge the relative autonomy of the state within the limits imposed by its participation in the societal division of labour and by the given potential for modification of the latter at any particular evolutionary epoch. However, in *Social Origins*, unlike *Soviet Politics*, he pays little attention to the cultural or ideological predispositions of those who exercise the power intrinsic to the state.

The impact of the above gaps in Moore's application of the theoretical approach he had developed by the time he wrote *Social Origins* is especially evident in his chapters on England and India. These are, respectively, the first and the last of the case studies and, in turn, the shortest and the longest. The brevity of the English case study surely reflects Moore's willingness to accept relatively uncritically that, in the nineteenth century, 'parliamentary democracy established itself peacefully and broadened down from precedent to precedent' (p.29). This last phrase is uttered by Moore without any hint of sarcasm.[9] No single point made by Moore in his discussion of nineteenth-century England is by itself outrageous or without some degree of empirical anchorage. However, the audacity of disposing in a few brief pages with a period whose social and political characteristics were already a fiercely controversial issue among scholars at the time when Moore was writing, and to do so in a way which blatantly resurrects Whiggish assumptions and terminology, is simply breathtaking.[10]

In the case of the chapter on India, the opposite complaint may be made. In the course of nearly 100 pages Moore attempts to solve a problem for which his scheme does not provide a ready answer. India had the institutional arrangements appropriate to a parliamentary democracy but did not appear to have undergone either the phases of political violence or the introduction of effective techniques of commercialising agriculture which he had found elsewhere. India's 'failure' consisted in the virtual absence of modernisation rather than the lack of formal parliamentary democracy. There is no want of scholarship on Moore's part. Indeed, his bibliography on India is far longer than those dealing with any of his other case studies. Moore's crucial omission is his failure to pay more attention to the consequences for India's political institutions of the ideological assumptions and related practices transmitted from the British colonial rulers to the native Indian intelligentsia. The space which might have been saved by giving more weight to this point could have been devoted to a discussion of the development of relations *between* India and Britain which would have clarified a number of the issues identified above. This, rather than the studies on Germany and Russia (which Moore has given us elsewhere), is the vital 'missing chapter' of *Social Origins*.

Two long reviews which notice, respectively, the failure to treat inter-societal relations systematically (Skocpol, 1973) and the neglect of the relatively independent impact of ideas (Lowenthal, 1968) are otherwise marred by an insistence on treating Moore's work as an example of Marxist scholarship. Skocpol, for example, argues that Moore's key causal variable is 'commercialization-flowing-into-industrialization' (p.11) without recognising the equal significance attached by Moore to bureaucratisation, especially through the agency of the state. Moore notices, as does Skocpol, that these economic and political processes may become 'disjointed' (Skocpol, 1973, p.31); there is 'no necessary connection between the two processes' (Moore, 1969a, 468). Skocpol also argues that Moore treats 'political conflicts and societal transformations' solely in terms of 'class-struggle and class-coalition explanations' (p.12) and fails at crucial points to consider 'political institutional arrangements as an *independent* constraint on class political capacities' (p.21).[11]

This last point is a little severe since for all its faults two points which are clearly made in the chapter on England are, first, that 'men who hold power do not necessarily exercise it simply in the interest of the class from which they arise, particularly in changing situations' (p.37), and second, that English industrialists had to discipline their workforce 'on their own . . . because the repressive capacity of the state was relatively weak' (p.32). Elsewhere Moore argues that in the course of 'revolution from above', as for example in Germany and Japan, 'The government has to become separate from society, something which can happen rather more easily than simplified versions of Marxism would allow us to believe' (p.441). Skocpol justifies her conclusion that Moore is a Marxist scholar with reference to the paper entitled 'Strategy in social science' (1958, pp.111–59), which I discussed in Chapter 2 (Skocpol, 1973, pp.1, 3). As I indicated at that point, my own reading has arrived at different conclusions. Furthermore, an examination of the first essay in that volume, entitled 'Notes on the process of acquiring power', indicates Moore's view that the independent constraints on political capacities, whether 'class political capacities' or otherwise, which derive from political institutional arrangements are very significant indeed.

Lowenthal reacts to Moore's reticence with respect to the origins of the ideological content of liberal-democratic ideology by assuming that Moore is a historical materialist (Lowenthal, 1968, p.259). The latter is accused of ignoring the contribution made by 'Western scientific culture'. In Lowenthal's view, this 'original revolution in thought' accounts for the unique characteristics of modernity and modernisation (p.261). He points out the significance of the American Revolution in creating a specific framework of legitimacy for the American state, for example through 'the dramatic innovation of the great written constitution itself'. Lowenthal argues that an explanation of Lincoln's public arguments about slavery should incorporate the significance of these prior innovations (p.267).

However, like Skocpol, Lowenthal jumps from a recognition of an important gap in Moore's analysis to an incorrect account of his overall theory. He suggests, for example, that Moore should have examined in his treatment of fascist societies 'the alternatives for action as they existed in each, and the possibility of choosing differently than the historical actors in fact did' (p.273). I have argued that such analyses lie at the centre of Moore's strategies of explanation and assessment. It is, nevertheless, fair to comment, especially in the light of *Soviet Politics*, that

> just as one cannot understand the origin and development of communist societies in Russia and China without Marxism, so one cannot understand the French Revolution (and the American Revolution and later Civil War) without Locke, Montesquieu and Rousseau. (Lowenthal, 1968, pp.261–2)

Although Moore is located in the intellectual tradition to which these latter writers belong, he fails in *Social Origins* to acknowledge the effects of that tradition upon political action. Lowenthal demands a consideration of 'The classes from which intellectuals are drawn, the relationship of fitness or unfitness between doctrines and the social reality they influence, the changes in thinking demanded by the actual turn of events' (p.260). As will be seen in the next chapter, Moore broaches all these issues in his earlier work but puts them aside in *Social Origins*.

It has been noticed that Skocpol and Lowenthal concur in treating Moore as a Marxist writer who neglects the distinctive contribution to social development made by key factors such as, for example, the state and intellectual activity. However plausible such a verdict may appear from an initial reading of *Social Origins* alone, it will not survive an examination, however cursory, of Moore's other major works appearing both before and since that book was published.

5

Terror and Justice

'Before I draw nearer to that stone to which you point,' said Scrooge, 'answer me one question. Are these the shadows of the things that Will be, or are they shadows of the things that May be only?'

Still the Ghost pointed downward to the grave by which it stood.

'Men's courses will foreshadow certain ends, to which if persevered in, they must lead,' said Scrooge. 'But if the courses be departed from the ends will change. Say it is thus with what you show me!' (Dickens, 1843, p.89)

It is tempting to introduce the allegory contained in *A Christmas Carol* at this point. Dickens, like Moore, pays particular attention to the two moral evils of terrorising subordinates and failing to consider humanity 'beyond the narrow limits of our money-changing holes' (Dickens, 1843, p.25). Both writers are aware of the common failure to recognise that present structural constraints are to some degree a product of past choices. 'I wear the chain I forged in life,' said Marley's ghost, 'I girded it on of my own free will' (p.24). Both Moore and Dickens believe that the future may be influenced by choices made in the present in the light of knowledge about the costs and benefits of alternative courses of action.

'The Ghost of Christmas Yet to Come'

In *Terror and Progress USSR* and in the last two essays in *Reflections on the Causes of Human Misery* Barrington Moore, writing in the early 1950s and the early 1970s respectively, points out 'the things that May be only' in Soviet Russia and the USA. Both in the Soviet study and in the two later essays, entitled 'Of predatory democracy: the USA' and 'Some prospects for predatory democracy', Moore discusses the potential for structural change built into existing social arrangements and the possible consequences of various initiatives or tendencies favouring change. There is an important difference of emphasis between the earlier and the later studies. Moore was writing about Russia at the end of the Stalinist era when there was considerable political interest in what was *likely* to happen in post-Stalinist Russia.[1] His study consists of a reasoned account of varying probabilities whose degree of likelihood is established with reference to the conflicting pressures built into the existing Soviet system. The 'organizing principle' of *Terror and Progress USSR* is 'one of showing the kind of situation that confronts different people in Soviet society, the way in which they see their situation and respond to it, and how their behaviour sometimes modifies it and sometimes perpetuates it' (1954, p.ix). The application of these principles in Moore's strategy of explanation in *Social Origins* has already been noticed. In the Soviet study Moore is primarily interested in identifying the *most likely* future structural developments.

By contrast, in the essays on predatory democracy in the USA he is primarily interested in identifying the probable costs and constraints relevant to the *most desirable* future structural developments. In both cases he is concerned with the relationship between practical possibilities and moral consequences. However, whereas in the former study Moore notices the moral effects of likely structural changes, in his essays on America he is concerned with the structural constraints upon the achievement of morally desirable futures and the moral costs of various possible strategies of achieving structural change. The methodology is similar in both cases and has a close relationship to that employed in *Social Origins*. A brief account of Moore's arguments will now be given, noting some of its implications for our understanding of the above-mentioned work.

Moore draws a contrast between the Soviet system and the social orders described by W. G. Sumner in which human behaviour was guided by 'folkways' rooted in popular custom (Sumner, 1960). In Russia 'The state has swallowed society' and dispensed with any heavy reliance upon popular consensus (Moore, 1954, p.2). The regime's freedom of action is limited by its previous decisions since the early twentieth century, by the internal structure of the system and by participation in 'a larger system of world politics that has certain dynamic tendencies of its own'. In fact, the closely interlocking character of internal and international activity is such that 'no one link in this chain of commitments can be readily singled out as the causal one' (p.5). Having established this framework, Moore identifies the instruments of control available to the regime. He notes a long-run tendency in the Soviet Union to incorporate technical bureaucracies, staffed by experts rather than politicians, and repressive controls, staffed by police and the military, alongside existing indoctrinating mechanisms. The intrinsic dilemmas confronted by the party leadership are identified in terms strongly reminiscent of *Soviet Politics*. What is new in this analysis is his preoccupation with the responses of subordinate groups within Soviet society, especially scientists and artists, precisely that class of intellectuals which he was later upbraided for ignoring in *Social Origins*.

He begins by acknowledging, as he did later in *Reflections on the Causes of Human Misery*, that 'the goals and standards of intellectual life' may clash with 'important beliefs' held in the wider society, producing a tendency towards conflict which has to be resolved by various social mechanisms in many kinds of societies (1954, pp.98–9; 1972, pp.90–2). Moore then identifies five premises implicit in the Soviet attitude towards intellectual activity. First, a materialist assumption that the external world exists independently of the human mind leads to a rejection of the view that scientific theories are the product of spontaneous imagination. Second, there is an objection to 'formal' theorising which makes no reference to objective reality. Third, the verification of theoretical propositions is held to consist in practice itself, the successful manipulation of external reality. Thus art must be judged in terms of its social consequences. Fourth, intellectual activity is believed to be unavoidably partisan as a consequence of its social and political effects.

Finally, while it is recognised that new truths may be substituted for old truths in the course of intellectual activity, this process is held to be preserve of political decision-making by the party leadership acting upon the authority vested in them by Marxism-Leninism. The final premise derives from the fact that

> Unlike another great and more tragic stream of Western thought, the Bolsheviks do not, and perhaps cannot, fully realize the instrumental nature of scientific knowledge, since they

try to make science the anchor of their total belief system. In this blind spot the Communist viewpoint is no different from that of its more simple rationalist critics. (Moore, 1954, p.112)

In his subsequent treatment of the responses of artists and scientists to the regime, Moore distinguishes between outright opposition, instrumental careerism, escapism, apathy and enthusiastic compliance. The goal which all these strategies are intended to achieve is 'some minimal degree of autonomy within the system' (p.153).

In Moore's view the fundamental problem facing the Soviet leadership in the early 1950s is to find a balance between power, rationality and tradition as means of social co-ordination. The totalitarian principle of emphasising power alone suffers from the absence of any higher philosophical maxim by which the allocation of power may be justified or guided. In fact, the unavoidable process of distributing functions and rewards under a totalitarian regime tends to create the conditions for a stratification system to emerge which would undermine the freedom of the totalitarian ruler. Such a tendency is also encouraged by the extreme social separation between the political elite and the people and by existing hostilities between national groups, Russian and non-Russian, within the Soviet Union. The emergence of a more developed stratification system would represent a move towards the principle of tradition. In such circumstances groups would derive a significant degree of autonomy and cultural distinctiveness from the enjoyment of property and privileges which they could pass on to their children. Such a society would be less susceptible to rapid change or bureaucratic regulation.

The objective of organising economic production and social co-ordination effectively encourages the allocation of functions to people whose authority is based upon the principle of rationality, i.e. competence to operate procedures which produce desired effects within a specific sphere. The extension of rationality contradicts the totalitarian desire to avoid acknowledging the existence of clearly defined spheres of competence outside the political elite's realm of arbitrary command.

Moore argues that a tendency towards tradition is evident in the education system, with its elements of 'Ritual, etiquette, and the development of attitudes of veneration for the past' at the expense of 'critical study of basic principles' (p.209). However, tendencies towards rationality are also present, expressed for example in the values of meritocracy. Movement towards either rationality or tradition would place the party hierarchy's control over knowledge and culture under threat. However, the cynicism about values which would be engendered at strategic points by a complete adherence to the power principle is also potentially damaging. International relations are relevant to Moore's argument since any movement in a traditional direction would require a relaxation of the pressure for industrial growth to support the military machine. Totalitarian elements, Moore believes, are very likely to persist. They are not explicable simply in terms of the dictates of international relations but are intrinsic to Marxist doctrine, Russian history and, indeed, Russian psychology (pp.20, 228).

It is interesting to notice, nearly three decades after *Terror and Progress USSR* was written, that recent scholarship has in fact emphasised both the elements of technical rationality in the administration of Soviet power and the traditional or ritualistic aspects of Soviet pratice with respect to, for example, the family, the education system and stratification (e.g. Lane, 1978, pp.275, 279, 370, 422, 507; Lane, 1976, p.211; Lane, 1981, *passim*).

Predatory democracy

In his discussion of Russia, Moore argues that because of certain costs and structural constraints it would not be *possible* in practice for the Soviet regime to maintain the morally undesirable kind of totalitarian social order which many Americans fear that the Russian leadership continues to want. Ironically, turning a similar analytical lens towards the USA nearly two decades later Moore finds that many Americans do not actually *want* the morally desirable kind of social order towards which he believes it might be possible for them to move if certain costs and structural problems are, respectively, acknowledged and overcome.

'Predatory' political authority is a term whose implications are explored in *Injustice* but it may be summarised as meaning a form of political authority which to a significant extent treats people as victims (1978, pp.440–9). Moore's two essays on predatory democracy, which focus upon American society, are significant in three respects. First, his comments on forms of political change and political ideals represent some important developments in his thought beyond the position reached in *Social Origins*. Second, from this new position Moore is able to mount an effective critique of the view that 'bourgeois democracy', the rising star in *Social Origins*, is necessarily bound by its structural characteristics to engage in a destructive global policy of war and waste. Third, he examines the possibility, likelihood and costs of various types of social change tending to lead towards or away from a decent society, one he labels as 'liberalism-with-a-difference' (1972, p.156).

The kind of society just mentioned would have the freedoms described in *Social Origins*. Furthermore, within such a society military expenditure would be reduced and scientific effort would be redirected towards humane ends. There would be an active public debate over goals, an end to wasteful consumerism, an increase in public services and a drastic attack on urban and rural poverty (pp.156–7). Although in *Social Origins* Moore had stressed the importance of the political power achieved by the bourgeoisie in England, France and the USA in bringing about democracy, he now declares, albeit in a footnote:

> There are grounds for holding that these ideals have much less to do with capitalism and the rise of the bourgeoisie than has often been supposed. It is at least conceivable, therefore, that in the future the essence of liberalism could survive the demise of capitalism. (Moore, 1972, p.113)

He also develops his position slightly on fascism. Summarising his argument in *Social Origins* he adds: 'By now, however, these aspects may not be crucial. Furthermore, adequate substitutes may arise' (p.152). In particular, he points to the anger of the 'little man' who feels threatened by attacks on the status quo in which his small stake is invested. Such sentiments represent the capacity for steely resistance which lies behind any mere lack of demand for reform (pp.152–4).

On the question of revolutionary change, Moore presents the fascinating idea that revolution (as opposed to simple revolt) is both a concept and a possibility whose historical epoch has been relatively brief (cf. Kumar, 1976). Revolution in this sense presupposes the idea of not only destroying the existing order but also creating a new one (Moore, 1972, pp.169–70). This argument was implicit in *Social Origins* and may indeed be seen to fit well within Moore's overall evolutionary view (1969a, p.427). However, another point which emerges clearly in these essays is the significant part played by the intelligentsia in undermining the legitimacy of regimes before revolution takes place. Indeed, Moore declares:

> Religious and intellectual currents do have an inherent dynamic of their own in the sense that a given system of ideas tends to rule out some types of question and promote others. It also seems likely, though this point is less certain, that some intellectual systems because of their strictly intellectual structure – the categories they use and the questions that derive from these categories – are more prone to internal development and change than others. (Moore, 1972, p.172)

He insists that although 'human societies do not simply secrete their own appropriate ideologies', ideas have to 'make sense in terms of the daily experience of human beings'. Established ideas may, indeed, cease to make sense or provide emotional security to people trying to orient themselves in the world:

> On this score a society may be ready for ideas that do not put in an appearance, or at least do not appear for a long time. When the ideas do appear, sometimes from the outside, they may spread like wildfire. Likewise ideas may be available, let us say, among tiny groups of isolated thinkers, for a long time without any effect because the situation is inappropriate for their reception. At any given moment therefore human thought may be considerably in advance of, or well behind, the possibilities for human action. (Moore, 1972, p.172)

One feature of these essays which is strongly reminiscent of *Social Origins* is Moore's habitual resort to the English case as a storehouse of favourable or comforting examples. Had not England moved towards a peaceful reformist democracy from a 'relatively repressive base line' in the early nineteenth century which was similar in many respects to contemporary America? (p.155). Had not the Philosophical Radicals in the 1830s skilfully exploited the perceived threat of popular violence as a means of persuading a regime anxious not to lose its legitimacy that reform was necessary? (p.163) Moore draws upon Joseph Hamburger's *James Mill and the Art of Revolution* (1963) when discussing the use of such tactics. Confronted with the 'portrait of English liberalism as the grinning hypocrite sitting upon the backs of those who in turn wielded the lash over plantation slaves and created the discipline of the machine', Moore shies away from it. He adopts the parodying tone exemplified above, and insists that such a portrait fails to capture 'the essential truth, the real relationship among the various factors'. It rests, he writes, upon 'the dubious assumption' that all trade is cheating and ignores the capacity of machines to satisfy human wants (pp.165–6). Moore's argument at this point would have been more persuasive if he had taken seriously the proposition that Britain's external relations, which in the nineteenth century continued to entail a significant degree of violence and repression, were as intimately connected with that society's internal development as they were in the case of, say, twentieth-century Russia.

The principal object of the first of these two essays is to distinguish between fact and unestablished assertion in the radical critique of the American government's exploitative and repressive policies abroad and its failure to reduce poverty at home. His intellectual strategy basically consists in identifying the logical steps in the arguments presented by Kolko, Magdoff, Marcuse, Baran and Sweezy, presenting data inconsistent with their analyses, and making a series of counter-assertions which are based upon conclusions arising from his own empirical work. Moore is sceptical of the assertion that exploitation and poverty at home and abroad are a *necessary* consequence of American capitalism in the late twentieth century. He displays his habitual caution in making specific assertions about the interplay between domestic and international structures. However, as pointed out in Chapter 3, Moore believes that imperialist tendencies are a common feature of not only early and late capitalist societies but also 'all sorts of precapitalist societies' (1967, p.406). This point is made not in order to dispose of the case for change but rather to redirect the attack towards the factor which Moore sees as crucial: the lack of motivation to bring about structural changes which are intrinsically possible. Such changes could occur, he believes, through a reform of the institutions of bourgeois capitalism within the framework of liberal ideals which became predominant as the bourgeoisie rose to power.

In a stance consistent with his entire approach, Moore is protesting about the Marxist tendency to treat American capitalism and its attendant liberal ideology in the late twentieth century as representing the only form of capitalism and the only form of liberalism possible in that society at that stage of social evolution. He is opposing the radicals' undiscriminating insistence that the social arrangements of contemporary American society are equally rigid in all parts. This attitude, he believes, results in a failure to recognise the effects of human apathy and of acquiescence by men and women in arrangements which are apparently favourable to themselves but which do harm to others. In effect Moore is requiring that we recognise the imperfections of men and women as well as those of the system. He proposes that practical strategies for change must recognise the possibility of exercising rational human choice. This capacity may be exercised in ways which do not lead towards social disintegration but which accept the medium-term costs of change in order to avoid the still greater costs of continuing without change. Moore's role has been that of furnishing 'the critique within the critique'. His stance expresses an austere rather than a romantic radicalism and is conservative only in so far as he is pessimistic about the degree of creative potential residing in social chaos.

At the time that Moore is writing the most likely outcome of existing trends within and between societies is, in his view, the collapse of political authority and accepted codes of social behaviour. Moore's recognition of this prospect may well have been one of the motivations behind his subsequent work culminating in *Injustice*. However, three other prospects for predatory democracy are discussed. The possibility of a reactionary or fascist development has already been mentioned. The reformist strategy leading towards 'liberalism-with-a-difference' through the institutional reforms described above would, believes Moore, encounter serious obstacles. These include the guild-like propensities of threatened occupational groups and the difficulty of bringing 'unemployables' into an orderly society in a way which gives them self-respect. Even more formidable is the difficulty of persuading the existing elite not only to make material concessions but also to 'change its social basis and function in a less repressive direction' (p.160). In previous periods, the transformation of elites had been associated with 'some new and growing social function comparable to capitalist industry in the nineteenth century', but Moore sees no such prospect on the horizon (p.158). The unpredictability of external relations also poses a problem since the active pursuit of world hegemony is probably incompatible with a liberal society (p.164). Nevertheless, he concludes: 'America is certainly powerful enough and rich enough to afford a great deal of social experimentation if that is what the mass of the people want' (p.167).

All other prospects seem worse to Moore, including revolutionary endeavours. Following an analysis of the way such events have occurred in the past, which is largely reminiscent of *Social Origins*, Moore adds that there has 'never been any such thing as a long-term revolutionary mass movement in an urban environment' (pp.179–80). The atomising effects of the work situation and the incorporating effects of socio-economic, legal and political arrangements have cut off this possibility. Rural movements have the advantage of being able to create 'liberated areas' which undermine the legal order, a strategy not possible in the ghettoes which have much denser relations of interdependence with the rest of society. He concludes this analysis with a critique of the strategy of effecting revolutionary changes through a progressive extension of 'community control'. His fundamental point is that the revolutionary bases thus created would be plagued both by their irreducible dependence on the complicity of the other parts of a differentiated social order and by the inherent weaknesses of the anarchist tradition. In effect, Moore is arguing that all such revolutionary dreams divert men and women from serious consideration of the actions which are necessary if they wish, like Scrooge contemplating his future grave, to 'sponge away the writing on this stone'. The essence of Moore's message seems to be the moral which was driven home by Dickens. Only if people awake reformed in spirit will they find that the Ghost of Christmas Yet to Come has 'shrunk, collapsed, and dwindled into a bedpost' (Dickens, 1843, p.90).

The social bases of obedience and revolt

In *Soviet Politics* Barrington Moore recounts the following anecdote:

Ciliga, an anti-Stalinist to the core, tells the story of a man sent to organize the health services of a little village in the province of Leningrad. This person was deeply moved by the gratitude of the collective farmers, who were stupified by the thought that the city had considered their plight and that the Leningrad city hospital had furnished, free of charge, medical equipment and beds for the village *créche*. Commenting on the crowd of peasants gathered round the newly organized medical centre, Ciliga's friend remarked, 'This is the first time in my life that I have felt myself useful to the people. (Moore, 1950, p.245)[2]

A concern with the moral implications of reciprocity is latent in Moore's earliest work. It is the central theme of *Injustice*. On the basis of my analysis over the last few chapters it is possible to reconstruct some elements of the process by which Moore arrives at this latter point. In *Soviet Politics* he shows that a regime enforced through repressive totalitarian techniques is perfectly capable of meeting the functional requirements of managing industralisation and maintaining its power. He demonstrates that the ways in which these tasks are carried out are explicable in terms of the interplay between the constraints of social reality and the (often ambiguous) imperatives of the legitimising ideology. Moore's analysis has the sharp cutting edge peculiar to an outsider able to exercise empathy, controlled imagination and skilful scholarship.

In *Social Origins* Moore argues that the responses of rural classes to the disruption or threatened disruption of their established forms of life produced structural consequences which contributed in very important ways to the realisation of democratic and dictatorial forms of political regime in industrialising societies. However, his powerful historical and sociological analyses are hampered by the absence of clearly specified moral criteria by which the political arrangements of liberal democracy are to be judged. In particular there is little or no discussion of the effects of such political arrangements upon the practical conduct of human relationships. The nearest approach to the specification of moral criteria is the remark, made briefly and belatedly, that in democracies the 'underlying population' have a share in enacting 'just and rational' rules (p.414).

In *Reflections on the Causes of Human Misery*, Moore is

directly concerned with moral consequences at the human level. His categorial distinctions are made with reference not to types of political arrangements, as in *Social Origins*, but to types of misery. Analysis of the latter produces the conclusion that certain liberal democracies might indeed be responsible for causing human misery on a wide scale. By this point in his work Moore is stressing the large element of fiction present in the descriptions of socio-political reality proposed by both liberal and Marxist ideologies. He is also, as has been mentioned, beginning to generalise more freely about human nature and human societies. In particular the most relevant distinction emerging in the latter respect is between decent societies and societies based upon force and fraud. One prescription for a decent society is his proposed 'liberalism-with-a-difference' described in the preceding section.

In *Reflections on the Causes of Human Misery* Moore considers certain proposals to *eliminate* the causes referred to in the title and thus to abolish or at least reduce the level of human suffering. However, the analyses conducted in that sequence of essays repeatedly imply that the discontent experienced by individuals and groups is a response not so much to the *level* of rewards or penalties received by themselves as it is to *the rules by which rewards and penalties are distributed* among all individuals and groups in the society. Significantly, although he begins the first essay by reflecting on the causes of human misery, by the end of the penultimate essay he is paying attention to the possible consequences of 'moral outrage' (p.149). In other words, the ground has been prepared for a more direct investigation of the ways in which human beings assess the rules by which power is exercised, benefits distributed and penalties imposed within societies.

Moore's discussion in *Injustice* employs the notion of an implicit social contract which specifies the appropriate relationship which should exist between those who exercise political power and those who are subject to it. Unlike John Rawls, who derives the principles of his theory of justice from a hypothetical 'original position', Moore bases his theory upon an 'attempt to perceive accurately the forms of untrained popular reactions of life experiences' (1978, p.xvii). Moore argues that 'it is possible to perceive a general ground plan, a conception of what social relationships ought to be'. He continues:

It is a conception that by no means excludes hierarchy and authority, where exceptional qualities and defects can be the source of enormous admiration and awe. At the same time it is one where services and favours, trust and affection, in the course of mutual exchanges are ideally expected to find some rough balancing out. (Moore, 1978, p.509)

Although there is 'a really subversive form of criticism' with a long history which questions whether rulers of any kind are necessary and proposes instead that all reciprocal obligations should be freely arrived at, the most common form of reciprocity or mutual obligation

accepts the existence of hierarchy and authority while attempting to make it conform to an idealized pattern of how it should behave. Obligations are accepted but should be reciprocal in nature: for the obligations of the subject there should be corresponding obligations for the ruler, and the whole should rebound to the benefit of the community. (Moore, 1978, p.510)

This notion of reciprocity does not derive from human nature alone since people tend to want to come out better rather than equal in exchange relationships. Rather, 'the rules are the consequence of human nature in a painfully constricted social situation' (p.507). In other words, people have to co-operate with others, usually in hierarchical social orders, and through these rules they try to prevent an intrinsically bad situation from getting worse. They get very upset, therefore, if the rules are broken. The rules are indeed broken with frequency but there is nevertheless a central core of ideas about reciprocity, widely recurring through time and space, to which both rulers and ruled appeal to justify their actions.

Injustice is an ambitious, scholarly, densely written and frustrating book. I have presented the main conclusion above not as a strategem to spoil a surprise ending but in order to show that my critical response has not been engendered by an outrageously novel conclusion. Rather, frustration is generated by the fact that Moore has in effect written two books and sandwiched one in between the beginning and end of the other. Moore begins by distinguishing between, on the one hand, 'central and recurring elements . . . in conceptions of injustice' and, on the other hand, 'historical dimensions and considerations' (p.xiv). These are examined in the first and second parts of the book, respectively. He argues that the explanations developed in the first part concerning the relationships between conceptions of injustice and variations in human willingness to endure oppression suggest 'many questions that should be put to the German materials and some of the possible answers'. These materials concern class relations in Germany between 1830 and 1914. In the third part of the book he returns to the general issues of the first part and approaches some 'methodological and substantive issues that came to light through the introduction of a historical perspective' (p.xvi).

In fact the first three chapters of the third part, which mainly concern Germany (with a sidewards glance at Russia), may easily be considered in connection with the second part, as they will be here. The remaining chapters of the third part can and will be considered with the first part. There are, of course, important links between the issues raised in the historical analysis of Germany and in the other sections of the book. However, the latter may easily be considered on their own and as in some respects constituting a sequel to *Reflections on the Causes of Human Misery*. The lack of close integration between the two parts of the text, which others have noticed also (Sheehan, 1980, p.730), expresses the difficulty experienced by Moore in fusing together satisfactorily his moral analyses of political authority relations and his historical explanations of political change.

This difficulty is minimised in *Soviet Politics* since his focus is upon the managerial dilemmas confronted by the political elite. In that book Moore is very effectively 'thinking himself into' the Bolshevik elite's ideological and structural situation rather than passing moral judgement. *Soviet Politics* is, indeed, the most tightly constructed of Moore's major works. In *Social Origins*, the difficulty mentioned above is responsible for the disjunction between his powerful analyses of what I earlier labelled 'causal processes' and the weaker plausibility of his discussion of 'consequential processes'. In *Injustice*, finally, there is an uncomfortable juxtaposition between a well-documented and self-contained historical analysis of German developments and an ahistorical exercise in political theory.[3] This will be considered in turn.

The making of the German working class

The analysis of German history contained in *Injustice* focuses upon continuities, variations and transformations in the structure and consciousness of the German working class between the early nineteenth century and the early twentieth century. Moore acknowledges the influence of E. P. Thompson. The latter's writings had suggested that the workers in an industrialising society 'were capable of developing through their own experiences their own diagnoses and remedies for the ills that afflicted them' (Moore, 1978, p.474). He is also interested in the Leninist argument that revolution or 'liberation' could be achieved by a vanguard party based upon the working class. Without this leadership the working class would tend to turn towards 'pure trade unionism' (p.477). Moore begins with a cameo portrait of the 'respectable' but poor eighteenth-century German artisan who has no notion of social revolution and who sees his own suffering as 'inevitable'. His response to intolerable oppression is flight rather than resistance and he displays an 'affectionate dependence on paternalistic authority' (p.125). What was the fate of the form of consciousness this figure represented?

Through detailed and careful study of a wide variety of historical materials, much of it consisting of data which have not been previously exploited by historians, Moore analyses in the second part of *Injustice* a series of related topics. These include: the participation (and non-participation) of German workers in the Revolution of 1848; social and cultural trends in the working class between this date and the outbreak of the First World War; and finally, the reformist revolution of 1918–20, paying special attention to the culture and political behaviour of coal-miners and steel-workers in the Ruhr. In the first three chapters of the third part of the book he examines the following issues: the conditions responsible for the outcomes of the German and Russian revolutions of the early twentieth century; the possibility that the behaviour of Ebert's Social Democratic government in 1918–20 contributed to the 'suppression' of the historical alternatives of either stable liberal democracy or socialism; and the conditions of existence of the Nazi regime as an extreme example of the 'repressive aspects of moral outrage'.

More than one commentator has criticised *Injustice* for taking insufficient account of developments in the working-class family and other institutional contexts such as the workplace which shaped working-class culture. For example, Moore has been told by one reviewer that if he had explored further in these areas he would have discovered the existence of the collective ideals described by Raymond Williams, and by another that he would have observed the hegemonic mechanisms by which the dominant bourgeois ideology imposed itself (Tenfelde, 1980, p.744; Wiener, 1979, pp.164–5; Williams, 1963). In fact, Moore's work demonstrates that he is able to make a very large contribution to the growing body of recent work concerned with the development of working-class consciousness, culture and organisation in the nineteenth and twentieth centuries. This body of work combines careful situational analysis with sensitivity to the limitations placed upon human choice by the specific forms of the division of labour at particular stages of social development. The parallel with Thompson's *The Making of the English Working Class* has already been mentioned. Moore's discussion of the German workers' 'common liability to misfortune' recollects some aspects of Michael Anderson's work (Moore, 1978, pp.197–201; Anderson, 1971). Some other convergences with recent work will be noticed later.

Moore's objective is to 'uncover and assess the main causal links in a unique chain of events that has had powerful consequences all over the world' (1978, p.xvi). These events led to the failure of the German revolution and, subsequently, to the Nazi regime. Data on organised political and economic movements are only considered in so far as they show what was happening to 'ordinary workers'. By focusing on crises, Moore hopes to 'illuminate the essentials of so-called normal behaviour' (pp.119–20).

Moore argues that the crisis of 1848 was a product of sudden and acute economic failures which caused intense social distress. It occurred against the background of a longer-run structural transformation which was subjecting guild organisation to bureaucratic pressure from the state and the eroding effects of the competitive market economy. Both these constraints were aspects of the decline of an established social order oriented to a static economy and a hierarchy of 'estates' whose primary values were ascriptive. The latter institutions and assumptions were being forced to yield ground before a commercialising and industrialising bourgeoisie.

The patriarchal bonds between master and journeymen were rapidly weakening. A new proletariat of unskilled workers was coming into existence which was socially marginal. The absolute size of the latter class was less important than the fact that it was 'surplus to that particular social order at that particular level of technical development at that particular stage of historical development' (p.135). The recognised social positions at the base of the old order were, so to speak, overfull with people. New social positions which they could occupy did not appear in sufficient numbers until the latter part of the century: 'Thus one could say that industrialization solved the problem of the proletariat rather than created it. There is more to the issue . . . But it is correct to say that industrialization was a solution of some kind to the problem of the earlier and pre-industrial proletariat' (pp.135–6).

In 1848 the temporary embarrassment of the forces of law and order permitted some violent score-settling within the working class, but support for revolutionary action, or even strike action, was negligible. Most workers did nothing. The most common demand of the masters was for protection of guild privileges. Journeymen wanted their skill and effort to be rewarded honestly without artificial restrictions. Both groups rejected the inhumane features of the new capitalist order. Its oppressive features were, ironically, no longer defensible in religious terms following the successful ideological onslaught of the bourgeoisie itself. An increasing recognition of the human capacity to reduce misery was one aspect of a changing political awareness which, as Moore explains in typical language, produced new definitions of friend and foe (1978, p.167; cf. 1972, p.12). This new awareness did not initially take the form of militant nationalism. The necessary role of a strong state in implementing the workers' demands was obscured by the identification of the government with the workers' foes at home (1978, p.171).

Anglo–German comparisons

In commentary it may be noted that many of the strains produced by modernisation in the growing German cities of the early nineteenth century may also be found, in very similar form, in some English cities.[4] For example, in Sheffield during the 1840s there were complaints about rootless elements in the population, especially the youths who crowded the streets and lanes on Sundays and were part of the quasi-revolutionary mob which marched on that city in 1840. There were similar anxieties about the ineffectiveness of social controls over apprentices (cf. 1978, p.140) and about dishonest competition. There were, as in Germany, demands that the government should step in to protect the established but threatened industrial order (cf. pp.146–7). Alongside the songs of the Silesian weavers expressing hostility to the exploitative putting-out system of the new rapacious breed of capitalists (cf. p.143) may be put the works of Ebeneezer Elliott, the radical rhymer of Sheffield who directed his diatribes against the Corn Laws and all capitalist monopolies, and also the often subversive songs of Joseph Mather, the filesmiths' poet.

There are similarities between the less-than-patriotic nature of many of the German revolutionaries' response to the Schleswig–Holstein crisis (pp.168–9) and the vigorous attacks upon the British government which Isaac Ironside, the Sheffield Chartist, carried out through his newspaper *The Free Press* at the time of the Crimean War. Karl Marx wrote articles for its pages. In Sheffield, also, there was displayed the ambiguous mixture of radicalism and intense conservatism which Moore found in his German materials. In the English case these feelings were often combined in an intense hostility to 'outsiders' and preparedness by 'respectable' men, pillars of their local communities, to take actions which were a threat to law and order (cf. pp.166–7).

Returning to Moore's discussion of Germany's development in the twentieth century, three problems give shape to his analysis. First, in what ways and to what extent was the German proletariat either 'tamed' or integrated within the industrial order by the time of the First World War? Why did the political events of 1918–20 produce neither a stable liberal-democratic regime nor a socialist revolution? What bearing do answers to the above questions have on the success and character of the Nazi movement?

Having pointed out that before 1914 the German industrial working class was a very small minority of the population and disproportionately located in the smaller cities, Moore argues that it was divided into an 'intellectual elite' and an inarticulate mass towards which the former adopted 'a somewhat patronising stance' (p.191). The leadership of the Social Democratic Party (SPD) was 'in its cautious policies and occasional outbursts of rhetorical anger at the propertied classes reasonably representative' of a working class which was heavily coloured by its provincial and artisan origins and traditions (p.217). These traditions survived well in the large mechanised factories. Working-class culture emphasised autonomy, pride in skill and a recognition that wage differentials should reflect differences in merit. However, the critical edge to this consciousness consisted in a demand for decent human treatment which took the form of basic economic security and a raising of wage levels within the capitalist system. In so far as workers expressed 'public concerns' they had a hankering for 'political equality in a good old-fashioned liberal sense'. This outcome would entail a reduction in the power of Junker and business interests within the political sphere (pp.212–3, 224). These were not revolutionary proposals: 'From the demand for acceptance in the social order it could only be a very short step to a positive willingness to defend this order when a foreign enemy loomed on the horizon' (p.225). The education system tended to reinforce these patriotic sentiments.

In many of the above respects the forms of working-class consciousness described by Moore were replicated in English experience, in part because this experience was also informed by the afterglow of an artisan past and the incorporating activities of the upper class through the education system. Moore contrasts the strong communal traditions of mining communities in the Ruhr and the much weaker communal solidarity of steel-workers, drawn from a wider range of social origins. Again, evidence from Sheffield and South Yorkshire in the decades before the First World War tends to fall into a similar pattern to his own. Workers in the Sheffield steel industry, to a great extent immigrants from the surrounding areas, were 'an historical creation from scratch–without customs, collective experience, or memory' (Pollard, 1959, p.91; Moore, 1978, p.272). By contrast, many of the surrounding mining communities had sufficient solidarity to mount a far from inconsequential resistance to actions such as the lock-out at Denaby Main Colliery in 1885 (Macfarlane, 1976).

Similarities such as those suggested above between England and Germany indicate the importance of structural differences in the broader context of political and class relations within which the working class was located. In his analysis of post-war Germany

Moore turns his attention to those aspects. His particular concerns are the fate of Ebert's SPD government and the character of the revolutionary uprising which occurred in the Ruhr. In the wake of military defeat 'the old order was unravelling rapidly before everyone's eyes' (p.292). The business elite, temporarily denied the support of an authoritarian state, was tentatively negotiating a new understanding with the trade unions. However, Ebert's objective of re-establishing production in Germany was complicated by the veto in the hands of Germany's neighbours. Further difficulties arose from his government's relationship with, on the one hand, the revolutionary left who were demanding radical political reforms, and, on the other hand, the conservative force of the army which provided the main repressive arm of the state.

The labouring population, reeling under the disruptive effects of the war, contained at least three identifiable elements: a conservative peasantry who had no interest in revolutionary innovations such as the workers' and soldiers' councils; a radicalised section of the skilled labour force which had been given its head by the wartime concentration of labour and the eclipse of traditional authority; and a large proportion of workers whose objections to militarism ran far deeper than their hostility to capitalism as such.

Moore pays particular attention to the Ruhr, where a workers' Red Army was created which for a time took control of several towns. Moore's analysis of this revolt recalls in many ways his treatment in *Social Origins* of the peasant uprising in the Vendée. The Ruhr uprising was in several ways the obverse of the revolt in the Vendée, though Moore does not make this point. Instead of being a peasant uprising the tumult in the Ruhr was centred upon the urban labour force. It was directed not against a revolutionary government that had gone too far but rather against a government defined as reactionary which had not gone far enough. In the Vendée the peasants were attempting to defend established structures of status and authority. In the Ruhr the breakdown of such structures helped to make the uprising possible. In respect of both cases Moore presents with great skill an analysis which relates currents of popular feeling at the local level not only to persisting structural characteristics of local and national social structures and their interrelationships but also to short-term but devastating alterations within that configuration. The Ruhr uprising, which like the rebellion in the Vendée implemented the basically defensive demand that established standards should be recognised, was put down by the conservative force of the army. By such actions Ebert in effect made his choice between the possibility of working towards a more liberal or even socialist society and that of compromising with reactionary elements within the social order.

Moore argues that the failure of revolution in Germany as opposed to Russia must be explained with reference to a number of factors. These include: the much greater alienation of the Russian peasantry from the bureaucratic order; the far greater contribution of the Tsarist bureaucracy to shaping Russian industrial growth; the particular traditions and composition of the Russian industrial proletariat; the very different international situation of the Russian government in 1917 as compared with Germany; and, above all, the decisive effect of the breakdown in the Tsarist forces of repression. The politics of the revolutionary party in Russia before the collapse of the Tsarist regime were far less significant than Lenin's decisive ability to exploit a fluid revolutionary situation. Also significant was the new regime's capacity to find some kind of solution for the fundamental problem of revolutions in agrarian societies – that of managing relations between the city and the countryside.

Historical alternatives

The key chapter in the analysis of German historical development concerns 'the suppression of historical alternatives'. Moore applies the strategy of analysis which has already been noticed in the first section of this chapter with respect to Russia in the 1950s and the USA in the 1970s. What prospects, asks Moore, were there in post-war Germany for the establishment of a stable liberal democracy or even a socialist regime?[5] Through the marshalling of available data and the application of systematic logic Moore seeks to explain why these outcomes did *not* occur. Part of Moore's answer is that sustained mass support for radical change was 'in the wrong places', notably in the Ruhr rather than the capital. Furthermore, the ease with which the old order was overthrown placed few restraints upon quarrelling and subsequent polarisation within the ranks of the left: 'Hence the old order in this largely abortive revolution was able to rely on the "responsible" moderates to do *its* dirty work, that of suppressing radicalism' (p.396).[6] This latter process, it may be noticed, reverses the pattern observed by Moore in the English revolution during which desperate radicals did the 'dirty work' of attacking the bastions of the old order.

Moore adds, however, that 'Relatively slight changes in timing and tactics in this fluid situation could . . . have brought about quite different consequences.' If there had been 'slightly different changes in leadership and tactics all round', if Ebert had used the threat of unleashed radicalism as a means of extracting more concessions from the old guard, then 'not only Germany but the rest of the world would have been spared enormous tragedies' (p.397). Again the implicit reference to English experience during the early 1830s, when the Reform Bill was arguably won with just such tactics, may be noticed. A major consequence of Moore's analysis is to make a moral judgement of Ebert and his colleagues relevant since they had a *choice* of tactics.

However, as Moore points out, a moral judgement must depend upon accurate assessment of the historical and other structural limitations within which the relevant actors were operating. It is thus worth paying attention to the methodology which Moore recommends. He grasps with both hands the nettle of historical determinism, especially its implication for the notion of moral and political responsibility. Moore argues that when social processes are compared 'some causes can be more important than others and . . . the relative significance of causes may change' (p.378). Among these causes are those identified with 'the application of human effort and intelligence'. Such causes 'can make a difference in human affairs'. In fact, 'the results of human intelligence and human effort have been continually entering and transforming the stream of historical causation as far back as the record goes' (pp.378–9). The extent to which they make a difference in particular cases must be discovered by historical enquiry and cannot be settled in advance of such investigation. People are morally responsible for those consequences produced by their actions which 'in the circumstance of the time these persons should have been able to foresee' (p.379). It is necessary to examine evidence which bears on the structural conditions impinging on possible choices, for example the decision to work towards either a liberal-democratic regime or a socialist regime in Germany after the First World War.

The relevant questions are all factual. Rigorous *proof* that any one specific alternative outcome was feasible (other than the one which actually occurred) is impossible to obtain. Nevertheless, questions may be posed which make it possible in principle to *disprove* that such an alternative outcome was feasible. The questions suggested by Moore in connection with the issue of whether an alternative policy could have been applied by Ebert are as follows:

(1) In these specific circumstances what concrete steps would such a policy imply? (2) What were the obstacles to carrying it out? Were they real or imaginary obstacles? How can we tell? (3) On what resources in the existing order could such a policy draw? What do we know about the working or nonworking of institutional arrangements, and the situation and predisposition of various sectors of the population during this period that would enable us to draw tenable inferences about the policy? (4) If there should be enough evidence to support the view that the policy was indeed feasible, why then did it fail of adoption? Did nobody in power think of it, and if that is the case, what are the reasons for this apparent failure? If those removed from the levers of power did think of such a policy, why was their position so weak? (Moore, 1978, p.380)

Questions such as this were not new to Moore's analyses. They may be found in his earliest work on Russia, as has been seen.

The morally abhorrent outcome to which the choices made after the war contributed, in Moore's opinion, was Nazism. This movement sanctioned and exploited a repressive form of moral outrage whose roots, argues Moore, may well be the product of a vigorous but frustrated work ethic (p.408). Such movements appeal to a wide range of social groups, as Moore shows through an analysis of the social support for Nazism. In its repressive ideals it exhibited nostalgia for a bygone communal order whose destruction may, in fact, 'be the most valuable achievement of modern industrial civilization' (p.420). Moore concludes by noticing that although their definitions of friend and foe may differ, radical movements of both left and right tend to glorify violence, use terror and adopt dictatorial forms of political management. At this point in his analysis, with moral concerns becoming more overt and dominant, the weight of argument shifts towards the concerns of political theory. At the end of his chapter on Nazism, Moore comments: 'But the choice is not between anarchy and irrational obedience. It is between more or less rational forms of authority' (p.433). His other line of argument which advances towards that conclusion is the subject matter of the 'other book' contained in *Injustice*.

Before turning to that 'other book' I want to point out that the above historical analysis complements *Social Origins* by providing a detailed analysis of an industrial proletariat as opposed to the peasantry. It also complements his Soviet studies by examining currents of feeling and ideas among the working class as opposed to the political elite. Seen in conjunction, these studies constitute an investigation, from successively different angles, of the dynamics of relationships *between* the elite and the masses, *between* rural and urban society and *between* the exercise of power, especially political power, and the implementation of ideas about the social order. Attempts to understand Moore as a Marxist writer and theorist overlook his primary concern with the relationship between 'the state' and 'the citizen' or, perhaps, the peasant/worker 'becoming a citizen'. He is above all concerned with the stake which 'the individual has in the existing order' and the ways in which that order and that stake may change or be changed:

By and large the industrial revolution has enormously increased the popular stake. The existing state has become the main agency, indeed the only agency, for the achievement of all purposes by all segments of the population . . . Put differently, without his own government the ordinary citizen is likely to feel that he stands no chance whatever of achieving whatever values he holds, whereas under his own regime he stands some slight chance . . . That aspect, however, is only the rational calculated core of support. To it one must add . . . wont and usage, the enormous influence that a modern elite exercises over the sources of ideas and the pattern of jobs and careers. The modern citizen is caught in a web of beliefs, expectations, and sanctions that tie him to the existing regime far more tightly than was the case with most of his peasant ancestors. (Moore, 1972, p.35)

A theory of injustice

The key to the work on political theory which is contained in *Injustice* is to be found in the opening pages of the chapter entitled 'Moral relativism'.[7] Moore begins as follows:

> Only in recent times has a fairly large number of educated people come to realize that there is not and cannot be any source of moral authority except human beings themselves. Even among educated people the realization is far from universal. With the decline of divine sanctions some influential thinkers for a time tried to substitute collective reifications with a teleological twist, such as Natural Law, History and Progress. These, too, failed to provide an objective standard for moral approval and condemnation. Historical and social analysis can provide powerful insights into what kinds of morality are probable and feasible under specific circumstances. Such analysis can also tell us about the costs in human suffering of different types of morality and who bears these costs. This knowledge is indispensable for informed moral judgement. (Moore, 1978, p.434)

Moore adds that a major obstacle to such judgements being made and acted upon is the prevalence of moral relativism, whether 'descriptive' or 'evaluative'. The 'descriptive' mode notes the wide variety of moral codes that exist and argues that each code is adapted to particular social conditions. The 'evaluative' mode encompasses the further generalisation that it is not possible to distinguish between these codes on moral grounds. W. G. Sumner, author of *Folkways*, is cited as a writer whose work expresses a tension between the two modes of moral relativism. Marxism exemplifies a particular form of descriptive moral relativism, one characterised by 'moral chauvinism'. In other words, Marxism asserts that its own revolutionary moral code provides 'a single standard of judgement' (Moore, 1978, p.435).

Moore's own objective is to provide 'a method of judgement superior to decaying moral absolutisms and prevailing forms of relativism'. Given that moral judgements 'play an immensely important part in human affairs', what statements may be made

about their nature? The basic proposition upon which Moore
bases his political theory is as follows:

> In any given case, morality and ethics amount to the rules that
> specific human beings have created and persuaded or forced
> each other to accept in order to work and live together. Poorly
> equipped for survival by their purely biological endowment,
> with the decisive exception of their brains, human beings are so
> constituted that they must cooperate somehow merely in order
> to stay alive. Survival, on the other hand, is no more than the
> absolutely minimal prerequisite for the other collective pur-
> poses served by moral rules. Apart from these purposes and the
> effectiveness or ineffectiveness that a moral code may have in
> both selecting and sustaining them, I see no criterion with which
> to pass judgement on any given form of morality. (Moore,
> 1978, p.436)

Many collective purposes have been recorded in different societies, continues Moore, some of them actually incompatible with
survival. Indeed, if human beings had been able to produce only
one kind of moral code and one kind of society man would have
become extinct: 'Variability is an essential element in the adaptation to different and changing circumstances' (p.438). Moralities
may become obsolete, as the example of Don Quixote shows.
However, Moore's intention is to search for observable agree-
ments with respect to the principles of social justice. He focuses
upon responses in the lower strata of various societies to shared
unpleasant experiences, particularly those associated with the attempted resolution of universal problems encountered in the quest
for survival.

Moore's discussion falls into two parts. First, he identifies universal problems of social co-ordination which are the subject of an
implicit social contract in relations between rulers and ruled. Such
a contract contains within it the norms of justice and the criteria
for identifying injustice. He also identifies certain constants and
axes of variation in terms of which possible forms of the implicit
social contract may be ordered. Moore proposes criteria of evaluation with respect to the allocation and exercise of political
authority and the forms taken by the distribution of rewards within
society. In a second and complementary discussion Moore con-

siders the circumstances in which moral authority is acquired by social orders whose attendant forms of suffering and degradation are on the face of it contrary to principles of social justice. Against this background, Moore then examines the psychological, cultural and social factors which facilitate the expression of moral outrage against injustice and action to overcome the unjust exercise of authority. These elements in Moore's analysis will now be outlined in more detail.

Social contract

Moore argues that human nature sets limits upon moral codes and also gives them a particular 'direction and impulse' (p.7). Human beings have a natural biological resistance to physical and psychic deprivations, including boredom, as well as a disposition to seek outlets for their capacity to be aggressive. However, these biological tendencies may be overridden by social conditioning and, furthermore, their expression is shaped by the imperatives of social co-ordination. The management of the division of labour and the distribution of its products have to be carried out in some jointly accepted manner; acceptance, in this case, means acquiescence or at least an absence of active and disabling opposition or non-co-operation. The principles expressed in three spheres – the allocation of political authority, the division of labour and the distribution of goods and services – may be considered as an implicit social contract. This contract justifies the forms of inequality which are generated by (typically) a mixture of coercion and free exchange. It expresses the moral code of the society concerned, a moral code which is the product of particular forms of interaction between three factors. These are: human nature; the social imperatives identified above; and, not least, the inter-societal context which places 'amoral' constraints upon political actors within societies. By a 'society', it may be noted, Moore means 'the largest body of inhabitants in a specified territory who have a sense of common identity, live under a set of distinct social arrangements, and do so most of the time at a level of conflict well short of civil war' (p.12).

Moore sets out in turn the criteria which are commonly applied to the moral assessment of arrangements governing the three aspects of social co-ordination mentioned above, criteria whose infringement produces moral outrage in terms which have 'the ring of universality' (p.27). He discusses political authority first. Political authority is 'in part a set of arrangements through which some human beings manage to extract an economic surplus from other human beings and turn it into culture'. He immediately adds, however, that authority is 'a reflection of the fact that the extraction of a surplus is not all there is to human societies, and that it is not the only source of culture'. Authority implies 'obedience on the basis of more than fear and coercion' (p.17). In return for the obedience and taxes of their subjects, Moore concludes, rulers are generally considered to be under a moral obligation to provide social order and external defence, contribute to social welfare and desist from abusing their position for personal gain. Popular attitudes to authority are irreducibly ambivalent since control of impulses is always resented. Excessive arbitrariness from on high is abhorred. However, there appears to be a demand, possibly stemming from childhood experiences, for a 'diffuse paternalistic authority' which the functionally specific forms of authority characteristic of modern society cannot satisfy (p.24).

Second, Moore turns to the division of labour. Attitudes to the division of labour have certain recurrent features: a tendency to associate control positions with high status;[8] a latent anger among those consigned to demeaning tasks; and a resentment by their fellows against 'idlers' in the lower strata. Finally, he refers to the distribution of rewards which is typically assessed according to one of two principles: either that the distribution should reflect an individual or group position in the status order associated with the division of labour or that everyone should have 'enough' to enable him or her to participate in the social order. The latter principle takes an egalitarian form in conditions of endemic short supply such as hunting bands. However, resentment against 'dog-in-the-manger' behaviour persists in complex and unequal societies. Fundamental disputes are likely over the relative validity of egalitarian as opposed to inegalitarian principles of distribution or, if differentials are accepted, over the principles they should express. These disputes are one aspect of the constant bargaining which takes place over the relative worth of 'equivalents' which are exchanged in a society. Such disputes are intensified by 'the contradictory requirements' which moral codes have to meet and by a natural human resentment at having to obey any rules at all (p.47).

In conclusion, Moore offers his own criteria for distinguishing between morally acceptable and morally repugnant forms of social co-ordination. He argues that the essence of justice is the application of 'rational authority'. In a passage which is highly reminiscent of his 'reflections' six years previously Moore writes:

> Rational authority is a way of advancing individual or collective purposes by granting certain persons the right and in some cases even the obligation to execute specific tasks and give orders to other people in the course of so doing. For such authority to be rational the individual and collective aims must themselves be rational. I will define as rational any form of activity for which in a given state of knowledge there are good reasons to suppose that it will diminish human suffering or contribute to human happiness without making other human beings miserable. (Moore, 1978, p.440)

Such authority may involve the exercise of specialised skill, as in the case of airline pilots, or simply of command where such power advances agreed ends. Compulsion is inevitable but 'the element of free, rational and deliberate submission has to be clearly predominant' (p.442). Those who submit should be in a position to judge the competence of those in authority. Despite the many problems entailed, 'By and large, the only way open to the ordinary citizen is to judge by results', a process which can only be made to work with any effectiveness in 'open and informed societies' (p.443). As a consequence rational authority is only possible in such societies. Within them, the only forms of elitism which are acceptable are those based upon the provision of status incentives to acquire socially useful skills and forms of knowledge 'which are difficult to acquire and hard to practice' (p.444).

In fact, a more common form is 'predatory authority', which is rational only in an instrumental sense and not with respect to ends. The extraction of a large surplus from an underlying population by a ruling elite does not necessarily make it predatory. The use of the surplus and the services received by the population in return are also relevant and enter into the moral criteria applied to predatory regimes. Such regimes typically lose their legitimacy long before being overthrown. The moral terms in which they are condemned furnish the goals to which revolutionaries appeal. In order to overcome such regimes force and fraud are necessary, means which inevitably provide the conditions in which new predatory regimes may arise. The very ubiquity of predatory authority makes it unhelpful to describe them as 'pathological' (p.447). In fact, the predisposition towards predatory authority is, Moore implies, as universal as the prospect of death. However, 'Doctors do not give up trying to prevent different kinds of illness just because they cannot prescribe pills for immortality' (p.449).

Disputes over the principles of distributive justice are also endemic. Sublimation of this issue or the adoption of egalitarian principles are two solutions which have not in practice been implemented by any complex literate society, partly because some important goods and services are intrinsically impossible to divide equally (p.451). As noted in the previous chapter of this book, Moore distinguishes between ascription and achievement as principles of distribution. He recognises the tendency for the latter to become more important in the course of modernisation and argues that it is in principle possible to determine on rational grounds the importance of the contribution each individual or group makes to the attainment of rational goals. Moore suggests that it is necessary for these principles to be continually explored and developed by 'competent and indeed gifted individuals . . . without let or hindrance from official and unofficial taboos' (p.453). He confines himself to noticing four practical structural consequences of periods of transition between the different principles of distribution.

First, in the early stages of industrialisation employers actually preferred a 'traditional' workforce which regarded the drudgery of labour as an inescapable aspect of its ascribed status. Second, the moral effects in terms of human suffering produced by different principles cannot be derived from the principle alone but from the interplay between the principle and the social conditions in which it is applied. For example, ascribed criteria depend upon reliable training in status norms and 'a regular and dependable supply of food and shelter', whereas the achievement principle offers a means of doing new things in a changing social order. Third, every principle of distribution discussed leaves *some* groups worse off, and they have to be persuaded to put up with it. Fourth, outrage results not from objective suffering as such but from 'the application of a principle that works to the disadvantage of substantial numbers of people, and particularly when the new principle deprives them of the results of hard work' (p.455).

This last point is developed in a different way in Moore's discussion of 'exploitation'. He wishes to confine the use of this term to situations in which human beings discover that the sufferings which are being imposed upon them are not justified. In other words, before labelling a situation as exploitative, 'It is always necessary to find out how people themselves judge their situation' (p.457). This insistence flows from his general position, which is that 'moral anger and a sense of social injustice have to be discovered and that the process of discovery is fundamentally a historical one' (p.15). His second set of themes concern this process.

The discovery of injustice

In the second chapter of *Injustice* Moore considers some cases where apparent suffering and degradation have not generated moral outrage among their victims. In all these cases suffering defined as 'inevitable' is regarded as 'just' in order that it might become bearable. The ascetic, according to Moore, is coping with unavoidable future suffering, perhaps associated with modernisation, by willingly imposing it upon himself or herself in advance and by lessening his or her desire for material and other satisfactions. Such practices are 'a functional substitute for revolution' (p.55). The untouchables, his second case, have neither the opportunity to revolt nor a set of values which legitimise such action. Like inmates in a concentration camp, his third case, they take pride in humble work essential to the social order. In the latter case the intensely interdependent hierarchy of the camp offers no outlet for independent revolt, though there are small pickings to be competed for. In such circumstances, as in a rather different way within the Nazi movement, moral sanctions tend to be imposed in ways which favour repression.

In what circumstances are tendencies favouring resistance to repression generated within societies? According to Moore, the signs to look for are, first, a discovery and rejection of unhappiness leading to a willingness to act against its causes, and, second, socio-political conditions favouring such action. Each major form of social order provides tests by which its legitimacy claims may be assessed. A theocracy has to persuade the populace that it can intercede with the divine. A military regime has to win wars and keep the peace. The case of plutocracies is more complex. A plutocracy finds the mere pursuit of wealth difficult to justify as an end in itself and tends to incorporate other goals. At the same time, regimes dedicated to other goals tend to become plutocratic because 'wealth is a solvent of other values through making it possible to purchase the good things of life' (p.86). One direction taken by plutocracies is towards welfare bureaucracy. Such political order may claim to be efficient modernising regimes, in which case their effectiveness is subject to judgement. Alternatively, they may claim to be just and efficient in their distribution of existing wealth, which offers other criteria of critical assessment, including the vigour of the work ethic (p.87).

The general point is, however, that such tests always exist. They provide opportunities for opposition movements to exploit regime failures and the consequent loss of legitimacy by proposing new goals and values which redefine friend and foe for the populace. Such movements also have to restructure forms of solidarity or exploit any restructuring which is already occurring in ways which enable the opposition to resist established rule. The social bonds between rulers and ruled and the meshing of their respective standards of legitimacy are thus crucial, more so than economic factors as such (pp.88–9).

Changes must occur in the mutually conditioning but relatively autonomous spheres of culture, social structure and personality. Focusing upon urban populations, Moore argues that condemnation of oppressive regimes and action against them depend upon a rapid improvement in a society's productive capacity (and therefore its capacity to reduce misery) as a result of technological and intellectual innovations. Other preconditions include a marked short-term increase in the suffering of the lower strata (especially through a disruption of its established social patterns), a split within the ruling class and the presence of non-proletarian agitators who are able to articulate grievances and suggest remedies which disrupt rather than confirm the status quo. Dissident intellectuals play a major part in helping to overcome the workers' tendency to revive an existing social contract which has been violated rather than establish a new one.

However, urban revolutionary upsurges have been rare, brief and fragile occurrences whose unpredictability mocks efforts to plan them. They are only possible if enclaves exist within which alternative social arrangements and diagnoses may develop. Within such enclaves intellectual ability in conjunction with moral courage and inventiveness of the order displayed by a Martin Luther may combine to produce a moral atmosphere which puts 'iron in the soul' of a regime's victims (pp.90–1). Moore recognises that the social mechanisms available to manipulate the moral atmosphere are unequally distributed within societies. Nevertheless, he argues that a very small degree of social support is sufficient to allow responses critical of an oppressive regime to come to the surface. After a rather inconclusive discussion of laboratory experiments by psychologists, he draws upon Freud for the assertion that 'there are evidently grounds for belief in an innate human tendency towards moral autonomy, manifesting itself through the processes of psychosexual maturation' (p.116). In fact, all forms of authority, especially predatory forms, impose frustration and produce the conditions for anger. Furthermore, adapting to repression entails the assertion of considerable self-control, and this response at the level of personality can be exploited as much by the revolutionary as by the oppressor. In Moore's words:

> Roughly the same changes appear to be necessary (1) for effective political resistance, (2) for adapting to the new discipline of the machine, and (3) for individual efforts to struggle up a rung or two on the social ladder. They amount to a strengthening of the ego at the expense of the id, the taming of natural impulses, and the deferral of present gratifications for the sake of a better future. (Moore, 1978, p.464)

Given 'the objective quality of suffering' and the fact that 'no culture makes suffering an end in itself', the 'absence of felt pain' in many cases must be due to 'some form of moral and psychological amnesia'. When cures for suffering do not exist such 'amnesia' may be 'necessary'. However, a feeling of inevitability which stifles a sense of injustice may also be the result of dependence upon 'generalised patriarchal authority'. Overcoming this form of amnesia requires a release from psychological dependence ('people have to grow up') and the creation of forms of social solidarity against oppressive authority. People have to recognise that economic and social trends may be creating new possibilities which make 'inevitability' an illusion.

The conquest of 'the illusion of inevitability' is part of the processes of modernisation and industrialisation, occurring first in the West. Moore makes a covert reference to the owl of Minerva as he remarks that now 'the process as a whole has come into sight' (pp.461–2). In fact his sweeping discussion of the concept of inevitability and its successive forms of expression has a definite Hegelian ring. He concludes that the notion of an inevitable sub-jection to the market's invisible hand has been the latest illusion to disappear. Modern liberal democracy, communism, fascism and liberation movements are all 'attempts to set the terms of a new social contract rendered necessary by the loosening of new pro-ductive forces'. In the absence of such a contract being estab-lished, Moore implies, these forces are being used 'for destruction on a scale without parallel in human history':

> But the kings new and old abide by no contract with their subjects. They kill their own subjects, each other's subjects, and on occasion each other. And they do it in the name of a 'public interest', a 'welfare' about which there is no agreement and which threatens to turn into a nightmare. One can only hope that the nightmare itself may be part of the universal illusion of a permanent present. (Moore, 1978, p.496)

One aspect of this latest illusion is, in Moore's view, the preva-lence of determinist assumptions which emphasise economic or ideational forms, functional imperatives, History, and so on. Moore prefers to think in terms of 'the contradictory forces that produce specific situations' and the possibility of morally informed human intervention. It is necessary, he believes, to overcome the subtle mechanisms existing in industrial societies which have the effect of institutionalising, taming or 'expropriating' the sense of moral outrage: 'This intellectual liberation from the inevitable may be one of the most important next steps we have to take' (p.500).

Summary and critique

Moore is in effect saying that a decent society is an objective justified in the light of reason and experience. The reduction of misery within the limits of possibility is a rational end. Most moral codes have in practice defined as just an exchange in which the hardships imposed by a ruler upon his subordinates are equivalent to the benefits he provides for them. Moore also suggests that this exchange will be regarded as unjust if it is perceived that more benefits could be provided and misery reduced through a feasible alteration of social and political arrangements. In the course of history the bounds of possibility have progressively been extended, as has recognition of this fact. A new social contract which would reduce misery is both morally required and socially possible as never before.

I have already argued that the 'historical' book on the German working class contained in *Injustice* complements the analyses of rural society and political elites to be found in *Social Origins* and the Soviet studies respectively. In a parallel way, the chapters on political theory in *Injustice* complement both Moore's earliest work in the 1940s on social stratification and his essays in *Reflections on the Causes of Human Misery*. In the latter essays it becomes clear that Moore sees the main hope for contributing to the reduction of human misery as being the development of a model of rational political authority whose parameters should be identified by a thorough empirical and theoretical exploration. Moore carries out this task of exploration in *Injustice*. He searches for the elements of a just social contract between rulers and ruled by examining evidence about systems of distribution and domination in a wide variety of societies. This wide-ranging survey of cultures from many points in time and space is highly reminiscent of his earlier search for 'the relation between social stratification and social control' (Moore, 1942). The statistical methodology of the early work has largely disappeared but the hankering for universal verities is still evident.

In *Refelections on the Causes of Human Misery* Moore formulates his moral calculus on a utilitarian principle which depends upon the assumption that no one would desire unhappiness, misery or pain as ends in themselves. As has been argued previously, the essays in this volume contain an attempt to come to grips with the effects of political arrangements (including 'democracy') upon the practical conduct of human relationships. This analysis brings relations between citizens at the 'micro' level under closer observation, but in the course of this investigation Moore is directed back to the examination of criteria of justice expressed within the political order as a whole.

However, in these essays, as in *Social Origins*, key analytical terms are introduced which are assumed to be self-explanatory and morally unproblematic as far as his readership is concerned. Just as 'democracy' is, by definition, somthing to be valued and striven for, so 'misery' is something to be abhorred and avoided. Both terms are descriptive and evaluative at the same time. In *Injustice* Moore continues to fuse together rather than separate from one another the descriptive and evaluative elements in his analysis. Crudely stated, he suggests that unjust situations are to be discovered by the existence of 'moral outrage'. Empirical evidence of human reactions will identify these morally abhorrent situations. Such reactions are to all intents and purposes universal. Moore's position is rather more complex than that, but the following quotation reveals its dependence upon the culturally conditioned reactions of Western intellectuals:

> An investigation with any scientific pretensions should specify the kind of factual evidence which would disprove the author's contentions. Thus compelling evidence against the view to be advanced here would take the form of specific examples of human behaviour about which (1) we as educated Westerners would 'naturally' expect a reaction of moral anger and judgement of social injustice, but (2) where the evidence showed no sign of such a response – indeed, that people generally regarded such situations as normal and natural – and (3) there were no indications of any social or psychological mechanisms that could inhibit or damp down such an angry response. (Moore, 1978, p.15)

Moore does not present any evidence which meets these criteria and believes that his interpretation of the historical data tends to confirm his own moral position. Some perils of this assumption and the approach upon which it is founded will be referred to in the next chapter in relation to the work of Quentin Skinner and J. G. A. Pocock.

In the pages of *Injustice* Moore is revealed as 'Enlightenment man' more clearly than anywhere else in his work. Responses inculcated by both the Christian and the classical aspects of that era's cultural bequest may be observed in Moore's attitudes towards, respectively, human nature and the state. With regard to the former, Moore suggests that the repeated and current failure to implement just contractual arrangements in societies flows from the fact that 'human beings may not have been particularly happy with what I have labelled the decent society'. Men and women are 'easily tempted by the fruits of civilization and on occasion obtain them by methods short of very hard labour – such as, for example, theft' (1978, p.439). The hidden image of the Garden of Eden suggests that Moore may be operating with a covert notion of original sin, a central theme of the Puritan tradition with strong roots in the U.S.A.

Perhaps it is not too fanciful to discern the cultural influence of a dualist Puritan theology which sees human beings as rational though deformed by sin, subject to universal laws but also having free will. These themes were also latent, as has been seen, in Moore's discussion of predatory democracy. Moore's attitude to human reason is complicated even further by his attempt, reminiscent of a transcendental approach, to demonstrate that notions of justice and rational authority are, to all intents and purposes, universal across time and space.[9] Such an assumption does not fit easily with Moore's Hegelian view that succeeding epochs are characterised by changing definitions of the rational. These difficulties lie at the heart of *Injustice* considered as a work in political theory.

Moore adopts the characteristic preoccupation of the classical writers on political affairs with the relation between the citizen and the state. I have already argued that this relationship, rather than the development of class structures as such, lies at the centre of Moore's concerns. Such a preoccupation is thoroughly rewarding when the subject is the Soviet Union, dominated as that society is by the central state apparatus. However, a major difficulty in applying this traditional approach in *Injustice* is that in contemporary Western societies the relationship between state and citizen is mediated by bodies such as trade unions, professional associations and business organisations whose presence considerably complicates the processes in which Moore is interested.

The kind of social contract to which Moore aspires in the political realm depends upon a recognition by rulers and ruled that they belong to the same 'in-group' and accept the same norms of reciprocity. Only in this way, Moore believes, can it be ensured that the consequences of social behaviour will be rational and just, restricting misery to the minimum degree possible. However, the fields of operation of the modern union and the modern business, for example, do not coincide with that of the state, though the effects of the former's activities may be just as profound upon those concerned. Furthermore, the loyalties of the company agent or the union member may well express the existence of 'in-groups' which encompass non-citizens and 'out-groups' which include many compatriots. The distribution of happiness and misery may be profoundly affected by the decision of, say, a French company to pull out of industrial production in Scotland or the decision of one group of workers to take strike action. Moore himself suggests these reflections by his remarks upon Sumner's distinction between the 'in-group' and the 'out-group'. He asks, with typical candour:

How does an American citizen who is a powerful executive in a multi-national corporation draw the boundary and in connection with what decisions? I confess ignorance about the answer. (Moore, 1978, p.12)

Progress on this issue would seem to require, at the very least, an examination of the growing literature on 'the corporate state'. However, this may not be attempted here since the time has come to evaluate Moore's overall contribution to the related fields of social science and political theory.

Part IV

Conclusion

6
History and Truth

In this final chapter Moore's standing as a historian and as a sociologist will be assessed with reference to a number of his contemporaries and, subsequently, his contribution to political theory will be considered in the light of the writings of some leading figures in this field.

In a recent paper Philip Abrams cited *Injustice* as one example among others of work by sociologists and historians which insists 'that, as a social relationship, class must be understood historically, in action' (1980, p.6). The analysis of class was, in his opinion, an important arena within which the problem of human agency had been confronted. This problem, in Abrams's view, underlies the differences between not only the 'two sociologies' identified by Alan Dawe but also 'two histories' which regard science and narrative respectively as the model upon which sound method should be based (Dawe, 1970; 1979). The revival of a new form of narrative which has occurred recently is one aspect of efforts 'to hammer out ways of analysing *process* which transcend the exhausted modes of narrative history and scientific history just as they transcend the exhausted modes of the two sociologies' (Abrams, 1980, p.9; see also Stone, 1979; Hobsbawm, 1980).[1] The new form of writing, whose concern is 'the movement of human agency as structuring', is organised 'in terms of a continuous confrontation and interweaving of narrative and theoretical matter' (Abrams, 1980, pp.9,11). Two important aspects of the new narrative mode are, first,

> an appreciation of the fact that structuring, the flow of action, structure and action, is mediated by consciousness, and that it is in narratives about consciousness that an essential item of evidence about the way process is constituted must be found

and, second, 'an effective appreciation of time as the medium of social structuring' (p.12).

The practical difficulties of producing the kind of analysis which Abrams recommends are considerable. As he notes, 'for most of us the rules of rhetoric – as distinct from the rules of logic – have still to be made clear and learned' (p.15). *Injustice* is a work by an author who has been applying the 'new narrative history' for over thirty years. The section on 'time and the sense of injustice' contained in chapter 14 of that work raises a number of the issues considered above, as well as others. However, *Injustice* also illustrates how difficult the rhetoric is to master. The strain towards consistency in the presentation of theory and the bias towards coherence in the empirical presentation of the structuring consequences of action tend to pull the text in different directions, as I tried to show in the previous chapter.

The social analyst who actually tries to identify what happens to specific social orders undergoing change through time must impose immense demands upon himself or herself. He or she must distinguish the separate elements, each with its own rhythm, in the complex and dynamically interrelated sets of determinants which enter into the 'movement of human agency as structuring'. These may include, for example, religious, economic and political developments. Having artificially separated these elements, they must be recomposed and evoked in terms of their impact upon and interplay with the motivations and intentions of specific individuals and groups as participants within (typically) asymmetrical structures understandable in terms of the division of labour and modes of domination. Having artifically isolated particular individuals and groups in order to specify the particular dilemmas they face he or she must recombine them as aspects of solidarities with tendencies towards coherence, disintegration and change. These tendencies are themselves important aspects of the 'sets of determinants' mentioned above. Furthermore, the analyst must be able to identify the interplay between processes occurring at different sites of social co-ordination and conflict ranging from, say, the family and neighbourhood networks to the national and international levels. Not least, he or she must be able to handle not only the modalities of narrative as a rhetoric of exposition but also the various logics entailed in comparative analysis.

The success of Moore's most well-known book, *Social Origins*, may be judged according to the author's response to these various challenges. It should be evident that, with some reservations as set out in Chapter 4, I believe that the challenges have been very well met by Moore. The same verdict may be applied to the 'historical' book on the German working class contained in *Injustice*. As in *Social Origins*, the analysis of process in the terms identified above was combined with skilful use of comparison both in the chapters on the Ruhr and in his references to the Russian Revolution. It is his capacity to mount concurrently a number of different but complementary strategies of analysis while still producing an eminently readable text which makes the work of Barrington Moore such a daunting standard by which to judge his contemporaries.

Barrington Moore and E. P. Thompson

If the historical argument presented by E. P. Thompson in 'The peculiarities of the English' (Thompson, 1965) had been incorporated in *Social Origins*, this would have given added stature to one of the few relatively weak chapters in Moore's book. In general and in many points of detail the approaches to history of the two men are very similar. There are differences, of course. Thompson has a close emotional and practical relationship to Marxist scholarship, whereas Moore has constructed his own personal bunker from which to launch a critique of liberal democracy and its antagonists. This difference between them is reflected in the 'significant others' whom they wish to influence through plain speaking. Thompson directed his 'open letter' of 1973 to Leslek Kolakowski, the dissident Pole, while twelve years earlier the recipient of Moore's 'open letter' on the New Frontier had been President Kennedy (Thompson, 1973; Schlesinger, 1965, p.267).[2] Another touchstone is provided by their respective attitudes to the work of C. Wright Mills. Moore regards him as a representative of 'the most tenable variant of the Marxist tradition' (1972, p.131), a tradition from which he carefully distances himself (p.132), but Thompson recognises in Mills a political as well as an intellectual ally (1978, pp.102, 115).

In *Injustice*, Moore acknowledges his great interest in and sympathy with Thompson's work and refers to him on more than one occasion in that book (pp.xiv, xviii, 18, 379, 474). There are obvious parallels in their mutual focus upon the consciousness of the working class in England and Germany, respectively. They also share an interest in the relationship between forms of class domination and the norms embodied in the juridical arrangements binding rulers and ruled. In *Whigs and Hunters* (1975) Thompson suggests that the norms and values embodied in English law imposed important inhibitions on the exercise of administrative power, for example in the early nineteenth century when the temptations to increase repression were considerable. Moore and Thompson share a considerable respect for the part played by the English legal and constitutional tradition in supporting claims to civil liberties.[3] Furthermore, Thompson's explorations of the notions of justice and reciprocity embodied in the 'moral economy' of eighteenth-century England anticipated Moore's concerns in *Injustice* to some extent (Thompson, 1971).

The notion of a 'predatory' or, more frequently in Thompson, a 'parasitical' ruling class or regime is also often employed by both writers to characterise the relations between those wielding social power and those subject to their domination (Thompson, 1978, pp.48–9, 56). Thompson exploits this notion in his discussion of the Soviet state. He notes the functions ('organizing production . . . defending the state against external enemies . . . and . . . defending the integrity of socialism against internal enemies') which 'the Soviet parasitism must perform, and must be seen to perform' and also the efforts which the regime must make to inhibit the development of 'a critical social consciousness' (pp.166–7). These same themes are central to Moore's analyses in *Soviet Politics* and *Terror and Progress USSR*. However, Thompson is conscious that such an analysis presupposes that 'social consciousness may determine social being' and is cautious in developing a 'thought . . . rather too metaphysical for a historian within a Marxist tradition to cope with' (p.167).

There are other similarities. Thompson and Moore both respond to Hegel's work with a combination of admiration and exasperation (Moore, 1958, p.108; Thompson, 1978, p.138). Each man finds some use both for the concepts of evolutionary theory and for the application of 'a subtle, responsive social psychology' (Thompson, 1978, pp.81–2). Furthermore, Moore might have written:

> And the bare forked creature, naked biological man, is not a context we can ever observe, because the very notion of man

(as opposed to his anthropoid ancestor) is coincident with culture; man only is insofar as he is able to organize some parts of his existence and transmit it in specifically human ways . . . for example, we cannot understand certain kinds of aggression independently of the ownership of property or nationhood. (Thompson, 1978, p.159)

Moore's exploration of the possibility 'that predatory moralities and social systems can in some objective sense be called pathological' (Moore, 1978, p.447) is reminiscent of Thompson's consideration of whether it 'may be possible . . . to translate certain notions of value, of good and evil behaviour, into diagnostic notions of psychic health or neurosis' (Thompson, 1978, p.150). All these similarities seem to flow naturally from their shared concern with identifying the potentialities in human nature and social arrangements and their stress on the importance of assessing historical change in terms of its effect on the quality of life, especially the reduction of human misery (Thompson, 1978, pp.68–9, 86–7).[4]

Thompson, like Moore, has 'a faith in the ultimate capacity of men to manifest themselves as rational and moral agents', a capacity which is expressed in the exercise of choice (pp.156, 171–2). Thompson's notion of 'historically emergent *potentia*' or the idea that 'given societies at given technological levels and with given social systems simultaneously disclose and impose limits upon human possibilities' is one already encountered in Moore (p.155). Both would accept that historical knowledge 'helps us to know who we are, why we are here, what human possibilities have been disclosed, and as much as we can know of the logic and forms of human process' (p.239). Thompson is aware that throughout history men have been 'placed in actual contexts which they have not chosen, and confronted by indivertible forces, with an overwhelming immediacy of relations and duties and with only a scant opportunity for asserting their own agency' (p.69). However, he resists the suggestion that there are 'laws of historical change' which have 'a metaphysical (and hence extra-historical) existence independent of man's agency' (p.122). The historical process is the outcome of 'a collision of mutually-contradictory intentions' occurring 'within a systematized context'. Man has 'a dual role, as victim and as agent' (p.152). Thompson convicts both Neil Smelser and Louis Althusser of offering history as a 'process without a subject' (p.271). In place of such abdication before an imagined inevitability he asserts: 'We *can* not impose our will upon history in any way we choose. We *ought* not to surrender to its circumstantial logic' (p.186).[5]

The central message in Thompson's open letter to Kolakowski, which has just been quoted, was also the argument presented in Moore's *Reflections on the Causes of Human Misery*. Thompson has arrived at this point partly through a critical examination of the implications of the Marxian distinction between 'the kingdom of necessity' and 'the kingdom of freedom'. Moore has engaged instead with functionalism, evolutionary theory and Marcuse. It is possible that their convergence owes not a little to their shared membership of a cultural tradition whose origins precede Marx, Hegel, Spencer and Darwin and which flourished in the 'mixed middle-class society' of eighteenth-century 'Hoxton, Hackney and Warrington, the Birmingham Lunar Society, the Manchester Literary and Philosophical Society' as well as Edinburgh and Glasgow (p.59). Perhaps Moore and Thompson incline, respectively, towards the classical and Christian modes of Enlightenment thought. Carried to the east coast of America and transmitted in (for example) the classrooms of Yale and Harvard, the Enlightenment tradition produced in Moore a man who implicitly compares himself to 'a pagan thinker' in 'the last phase of classical civilization', one who 'is sufficiently intelligent and humane to recognize that the Roman Empire was cruel and corrupt, that its rationale was nonsense which no intelligent person could take seriously any longer' (Moore, 1972, p.103). In the case of Thompson it produced a man who could be driven to 'minority-minded self-isolation' and whose chosen image is of being 'a representative of a residual tradition, like Old Dissent, adhering meticulously to old forms whose significance daily diminishes' (Thompson, 1978, p.182).

Whatever the reasons, Moore and Thompson write history from very similar standpoints. The methodology of both writers expresses a confidence in the independence of historical facts, an aversion to over-formalised and rigid concepts and a tendency to invite the test of falsifiability rather than assert positive scientific proof for their findings (pp.220, 78, 238, 232). Perhaps the most valuable section of Thompson's essay on 'the poverty of theory' is his 'brief intermission' on historical logic (pp.229–42). Without

entering into a full exposition it may be noticed that Thompson
regards the dialogue between concept and evidence, conducted
through the exploration of successive hypotheses and through
empirical research, as central to historical work. Historical knowledge, he recognises, is provisional, selective and defined by the
questions asked of the evidence but not therefore 'untrue' (p.231).
The true character of historical processes, i.e. '*practices* ordered
and structured in rational ways', and 'their intricate causation' may
be learned by historians whose misunderstandings or distortions
'can't in the slightest degree modify the past's ontological status'
(p.232).[6]

Thompson is taking his stand here not only with Marc Bloch but
also with Barrington Moore. Like the latter, Thompson makes a
distinction between 'objective knowledge' about the 'rationality
(of causation, etc.) of the historical process' and evaluative judgements about its 'significance' or 'meaning' (p.233; see also Moore,
1969a, pp.521–2). Thompson might easily be describing the strategy adopted by Moore in his analysis of 'consequential processes'
leading to bourgeois democracy in *Social Origins* when he writes:

> I accept . . . that if we select one set of possibilities among other
> sets as *potentia* this 'project is a decision about the choice of
> values'. But even here one might allow for a rational (but not
> eschatological) hope that the attribution of *potentia* is not a *post
> facto* insertion by the observer only, but is simultaneously an
> empirically-given and demonstrable possibility within actual
> historical process. That is, one proposition does not invalidate
> the other: I may say as a matter of 'faith' that I choose to
> identify with one *potentia* and not the others, and I may say as a
> historical investigator that the chosen *potentia* is one of the
> empirically-observable possibilities of choice, and I may add
> that I am, in my choosing and valuing nature, an outcome of
> this *potentia*. (Thompson, 1978, p.148)

In *Social Origins*, Moore's skilful comparative analysis of the
transformations in social differentiation attendant upon modernisation was weakened at important points by a failure to pay
adequate attention to the growth and penetration of liberal-democratic ideology within specific societies. In *The Making of the
English Working Class*, Thompson was centrally concerned with

the latter process. The repression and suffering of the period between the 1790s and the 1820s were experienced by 'freeborn Englishmen' who had acquired important elements of just such a culture. In his turn, Thompson has been criticised for paying inadequate attention to the 'objective coordinates' within which working-class consciousness took shape (Anderson, 1980, p.33). Indeed, Perry Anderson cites *Injustice* as a work which presents 'a more satisfactory treatment' of the problem of analysing the inter-play between human agency and structural constraints deriving from, for example, the mode of production. However, a full understanding of the approach to historical analysis which Thompson has been developing can no more be found by simply concentrating upon his greatest work than can Moore's distinctive approach be drawn simply from the pages of *Social Origins*.

Narrative history and comparative sociology

A major difference between *The Making of the English Working Class* and *Social Origins* is that whereas the former describes important aspects of a particular complex process in a single society the latter seeks to evoke a number of interacting processes through the extensive use of comparative analysis. The combination of two modes of exposition, the explication of process through narrative and the elaboration of general explanations (not confined to specific cases or societies) through comparative analysis is one of the trickiest arts in the practice of history or sociology. This is not to argue that comparisons are absent from Thompson's classic work. At one point, for example, he contrasts the communal experiences of field labourers, artisans and handloom weavers (1968, pp.233–346). However, the examples derive significance from their location within a process whose overall sweep is well established and treated as given by the time they appear in the text.

It is tempting to compare Thompson's use of such contrasts with Wallerstein's references to different societies in *The Modern World-System*. These latter derive their significance from their location within a broader context defined by a newly developing framework of differentiation. In this latter case the framework is 'the new European division of labour' whose outlines are well established in the argument before the detailed discussion of core, peripheral and semi-peripheral societies gets under way. Despite their many differences, these works by Thompson and Wallerstein both attempt to explain the development of new systems of differentiation and domination whose persistence, it is argued, has radically restricted the options for future development open to the collectivities trapped within them and structured by them. In one case the object of analysis is a structure of class domination within a particular society and in the other a structure of inter-societal domination. However, Wallerstein bases his argument upon a set of *a priori* distinctions between types of 'system' and concentrates upon the nature of system constraints rather than the experiences of those subject to such constraints (Wallerstein, 1980a, pp.5–6). In both these respects Thompson differs from him.

Moore's analysis in *Social Origins* produces generalisations about social processes which are justified in terms of a logic of comparison which is deployed in the course of his exposition. His approach may be contrasted with that of Perry Anderson in *Passages from Antiquity to Feudalism* and *Lineages of the Absolutist State*. In a recent paper entitled 'Comparative sociology or narrative history?', W. G. Runciman has re-analysed several of the specific historical cases cited by Anderson and produced very different conclusions. Through a comparison between Rome and China, Runciman argues that Anderson has failed 'to validate the propositions which would have to hold if large-scale agricultural slavery is to be accepted as either a necessary or a sufficient cause of the Western Empire's fall' (Runciman, 1980, p.166). Anderson also fails to 'show both that the subsequent success of Japanese industrial capitalism was due to its 'feudal' history and that it could not be accounted for instead, or even as well, by anything else' (p.168). Furthermore, he fails to justify his application of the term 'absolutist' to the English state before the Civil War (p.170). In Runciman's words, 'Anderson's commitment to an expected sequence leads him to play down the significance of the very contrasts which his own reading of the evidence has, quite rightly, led him to draw' (p.171). Runciman presents some elements of an alternative argument which, *contra* Anderson, emphasises the differences between seventeenth-century England and France and the similarities between pre-revolutionary France and pre-revolutionary Russia (pp.171, 178).

The object of Runciman's analysis is not to dismiss Anderson's work, whose importance he rightly acknowledges, but to indicate 'the unresolved tension within it between historical narrative and comparative sociology'. In the narrative accounts of particular societies, 'certain sequences are taken to be expected in the absence of special explanation'. Although several comparisons are made they 'do not constitute the organising principle around which his macro-sociological explanations are constructed' (pp.162, 163). Anderson's work may be contrasted with another book whose author, a student of Barrington Moore, deliberately organises her argument around a series of macro-sociological comparisons in order to justify a series of generalisations about social revolutions.

Theda Skocpol's work displays in full measure Moore's own tenacious commitment to clarity of analysis. This shared virtue and the considerable overlap in their historical and intellectual concerns make comparison between Moore and Skocpol a fruitful exercise. Two aspects of Theda Skocpol's argument in *States and Social Revolutions* are especially noteworthy. First, the occurrence of revolutions in France, Russia and China is partly explained in terms of inter-societal configurations which placed the state apparatus under considerable pressure in each case. Second, Skocpol indicates the structural significance of the distinction between the national and local levels of class and political organisations, particularly with respect to the aristocracy. Both aspects of her argument are developed through some illuminating empirical generalisations. However, the following comments are less concerned with the important substantive conclusions which Skocpol presents than with the methodology she elaborates and applies *en route* to these conclusions.

Skocpol's avowed objective is that of comparing 'selected slices of national historical trajectories' from 'an impersonal or nonsubjective viewpoint' in order to arrive at generalisable statements about causal regularities (Skocpol, 1979, pp.18, 35). Her chosen objects of analysis are 'social revolutions', which are defined as 'rapid, basic transformations of a society's state and class structures . . . accompanied and in part carried through by class-based revolts from below' (p.4). Her application of the comparative method consists of two processes: comparison of three examples of 'successful' social revolutions (France, Russia, China); and comparison of these cases with, on the one hand, 'unsuccessful' social revolutions (Germany in 1848) and 'successful' political revolutions which were not 'social revolutions' (England in the seventeenth century and Japan in the nineteenth century). The first type of comparison exploits the 'method of similarity', i.e. comparisons of cases which share both the explicandum and the hypothesised causes, though differing in other potentially relevant respects. The second type of comparison applies the 'method of difference', which is 'more powerful' (p.36). Cases are compared which are as far as possible similar to the positive cases but different with respect to the explicandum and the hypothesised causes.

Skocpol argues that she is presenting a 'structuralist' analysis, one which explains outcomes not in terms of the purposes or intentions of actors but in terms of 'the institutionally determined situations and relations of groups within society and the interrelations of societies within world-historically developing international structures' (p.18). Ironically, in dismissing Marxist schemes such as those of Althusser (p.6), Skocpol comes close to the latter's radical rejection of volition. What individuals or groups 'want' or 'choose' is seen as being of little epistemological relevance to the social analyst. In practice, however, she does not implement this approach with rigour. In the first part of her book she indeed focuses upon 'structural' factors. She argues, for example, that the coincidence of external pressures upon the state (especially military threats) and serious internal crises (especially peasant uprisings) produced a breakdown of the old regime's capacity to govern.

In the second part of her book, however, the 'thread' which she follows is the processes whereby 'emergent political leaderships' struggled to create and consolidate a new state organisation. She identifies the constraints to which they were subject, both at home and abroad, and explains outcomes in terms of their 'broadly similar exigencies, challenges and opportunities' (pp.161, 163, 173). In the Chinese case it was necessary for the revolutionary leadership to take active measures to bring into being the 'distinctive political capacities' which they 'accumulated' by their work among the peasantry (p.275). In effect, despite her structuralist rhetoric, Skocpol recognises not only the importance of the 'situational logic' confronting the key actors but also their ability to respond to it, exploit it and in important ways to alter it. Human agency plays an important, if unheralded, role in her argument (cf.

Himmelstein and Kimmel, 1981, pp.1153–4).

In one respect Skocpol's application of the comparative method is less penetrating than its use by Moore. In her exploitation of the 'method of difference' Skocpol quite deliberately confines herself to examples for comparison in which, despite several similarities to her cases of 'successful social revolution', both the hypothesised causes of social revolution and the outcome itself are absent. By citing such cases the initial hypothesis, already supported through the 'method of agreement', tends to be confirmed and the risk of encountering data which actually *contradict* that hypothesis is removed. By contrast, in *Social Origins* Moore typically uses the comparative method in order to test successive hypotheses, suggested in the course of his exposition, through two different procedures. He sometimes compares two or more examples in which a hypothesised cause is present but which differ with respect to the outcome he is seeking to explain. An instance is his comparison of relations between great landowners and industrialists in Germany and the USA respectively during the nineteenth century. Civil war occurred in the latter case but not the former. Alternatively, he sometimes compares cases in which the relevant outcome *is* shared between societies but various hypothesised causes are *not* shared. One example is his contrast between the state of relations between the aristocracy and bourgeoisie in seventeenth-century France and England. Despite very different antecedent conditions, democracy resulted in both societies. In other words, comparisons are mounted with the object of subjecting hypotheses to the test of data which contradict them.

One way in which Skocpol could have exploited this approach is by comparing her three 'positive' cases with instances of societies in which her hypothesised causes of social revolution were present but in which successful social revolution did not occur. One example might be Germany after the First World War, a case which has attracted Moore's attention. It was a society whose state apparatus had to a great extent collapsed, the managers of whose old regime had to a great extent retired from political life and which did experience the impact of class-based revolt from below. Germany became transformed, after a period of time far shorter than the gap between 1911 and 1949 in China, into the Third Reich. Whether Germany is assessed from the standpoint of 1920 (in the context of military repression of popular upheaval) or from the standpoint of 1945 (following the defeat of Hitler's 'dictatorial party-state'), this society may not be described as having undergone a 'successful' social revolution.

The above reference to Germany after the First World War suggests another analytical procedure exploited by Moore which Skocpol neglects. She does not consider the structural or 'historical' alternatives to successful social revolution which were available to her key societies – France, Russia and China – *at the points in time* when the old regimes collapsed. Her argument very effectively suggests that in 1789, 1917 and 1911–49, respectively, popular unrest without subsequent radical societal transformation was highly unlikely, as was fundamental structural change without violence. She also argues with plausibility, citing *other* societies at *other* times that in some cases class upheaval was unlikely to produce radical structural change and that in other cases such change was possible without the violence of class conflict. These latter alternatives were *not* available at the time of the collapse of old regimes in France, Russia and China. However, Skocpol pays insufficient attention to two alternative modes of achieving radical societal transformation through violent means which were indeed 'on the cards'. They were, first, military defeat and occupation by a victorious foreign power, and, second, colonial domination subject to resistance by a nativist liberation movement. The distinction between these two alternatives is in practice sometimes blurred, as the case of China in the early twentieth century suggests. However, both outcomes would have had the effect of violently displacing existing state regimes and ruling classes, replacing them with new ones. As both Mao and Lenin realised, the actual alternatives to successful social revolutions were probably either military conquest or colonial domination. The fate of Eastern Europe in the wake of the collapse of the Austro-Hungarian Empire illustrates these possibilities.

It might have been helpful if Skocpol had begun by locating the particular constellation of structures and processes characterising her three cases of successful social revolution within the entire range of empirical possibilities for modernisation. Successful social revolutions and political revolutions do not exhaust this range. To cite a formulation which owes much to Moore's influence, such revolutions are particular forms taken by 'processes of structural transformation which tend to increase both the resource-producing or energy-producing capacity of a social configuration and the extent to which this capacity may be realized by strategic elites' (Smith, 1978, p.177). Applying such a framework to the contrasting conditions under which old regimes in agrarian bureaucracies pass away, one might conduct a comparative analysis which asks: why do some old regimes become extinct in the course of social revolution, others in the course of military conquest and still others through the impact of colonial penetration? An approach combining Moore's sensitivity to the range of modernising routes and Skocpol's awareness of the importance of the external relations of states would yield rich returns. Furthermore, it may be argued within the framework of such a broader analysis that social revolution, inter-societal conflict and sequences of colonial domination have a dynamic relationship to each other when viewed within a global context (Smith, 1978, pp.181, 185–91).[8]

Like Moore, Skocpol is concerned with both the causes and the consequences of violent social upheavals. However, Skocpol's treatment of causation minimises the significance of human perception and motivation (as opposed to tendencies within economic and political macro structures), and her discussion of consequences minimises the significance of moral criteria (as opposed to evidence of changes in class structure and the organisation of the state). Two of the most distinctive characteristics of Moore's analytical approach are thus absent. It may be significant that Skocpol applies a comparative method taken almost directly from J. S. Mill (1888). In a sense, to move from Moore to Skocpol is to encounter in succession two ideals of scholarship, to pass from an eighteenth-century view of Humanity as the object of analysis to a nineteenth-century view of Science as the method of analysis. However, that is to overemphasise the differences between two writers who, in fact, arrive at very similar (and rather pessimistic) conclusions about the possibilities for overcoming oppressive political authority in the late twentieth century (Skocpol, 1979, pp.292–3). It is perhaps appropriate that Skocpol's final paragraph in *States and Social Revolutions* should contain an approving reference to Franz Neumann, whose work on the state was such an important influence on Moore's own early publications (Skocpol, 1979, p.292; Neumann, 1957; Moore, 1955, p.107; 1958, pp.132–3).

Theda Skocpol's work represents a vigorous and stimulating attempt to cut through the Gordian knot which Barrington Moore has patiently been attempting to untie. His objectives have been: to develop a way of arriving at generalisable explanations of societal development which recognise the interplay between historical or other structural constraints and human agency; and to apply methodological techniques which maximise objectivity while incorporating a moral or evaluative dimension in the analysis. As was seen in Chapter 4, Moore's style of presentation in *Social Origins* subtly combines comparative and narrative modes within each chapter, subjects the author to a continual self-interrogation, indicates the rationality of human choices in terms of the perceptions of the relevant actors, and consistently identifies the victims and beneficiaries of social change or the failure to change.

Moore's approach may be compared with the following statement:

> I myself feel that I am being thoroughly consistent and that my concern with history, with social science and with politics is not a matter of engaging in three separate, even if related activities, but is a *single* concern, informed by the belief that the strands cannot be separated, nor should they be if they could . . . I do not believe that there is or could be such a thing as value-free historical social science. Every choice of conceptual framework is a political option. Every assertion of truth, or heuristic theory, is an assertion of value. All good scholarship is polemic (but not all good polemic is good scholarship). (Wallerstein, 1980a, pp.vii, x)[9]

Despite some differences which will be mentioned shortly, there is a considerable degree of convergence between Moore and Wallerstein with respect to the character and objectives of social analysis. Both recognise that perceptions of truth alter as societies change (Wallerstein, 1974, p.9; 1980a, p.x), that objectivity arising from full and free discussion is a function of 'the distribution of social investment in such activity' (1974, p.10), and that 'In general, in a deep conflict, the eyes of the downtrodden are more acute about the reality of the present. For it is in their interests to perceive correctly in order to expose the hypocrisy of the rulers. They have less interest in ideological deflection' (p.4). Both also accept that although 'we are all irremediably the product of our background, our training, our personality and social role, and the structured pressures within which we operate', that is 'not to say that there are no options. Quite the contrary' (p.9).

The academic career of Wallerstein has some interesting resemblances to that of Moore. Both felt more at ease, intellectually, in the debates of the 1950s to which C. Wright Mills, Herbert Marcuse and Franz Neumann were major contributors rather than those in which the dominant schools of Parsons and Lazarsfeld were engaged. Both specialised in the study of social development in particular areas (Africa and Russia respectively) before achieving wide recognition for major works which traversed disciplines, societies and time periods. Both have been concerned with the particular contribution made by forms of commercialised or capitalist agriculture to the shaping of the modern world. Neither has been confined within either a Marxist or a Weberian approach and both have been equally scathing about the ideological claims of communist and liberal regimes.

The influence of Fernand Braudel and Karl Polanyi and also a concern to present an analytical description of long-term sequences of development in the capitalist world-economy since the 'crisis of feudalism' are, of course, distinctive to Wallerstein. The latter project is a major exercise in narration, an important part of Wallerstein's self-imposed agenda being that of 'redoing our historical narratives, accumulating new world-systemic quantitative data (almost from scratch), and above all reviewing and refining our conceptual baggage' (1980a, p.136). As implied previously, comparative analysis remains strictly subordinate to these objectives. The comparisons Wallerstein makes are often very illuminating, as is his contrast between Europe and China in the fifteenth century (1974, pp.52–6), but they are usually designed to carry further simultaneously a number of related narrative themes rather than logically produce the argument about the development of the world-economy. However, it should be noted that, in association with Terence Hopkins, Wallerstein has written one of the most sophisticated and useful reviews of methodological approaches to the comparative study of national societies which is available in the literature (Hopkins and Wallerstein, 1967).[10] As in the case of Anderson, the point to be noted is the persistence in Wallerstein's work of the 'unresolved tension' between comparative sociology and narrative history.

Like *Social Origins*, a book to which it has been compared sometimes favourably (Hechter, 1975, p.222) and sometimes unfavourably (Janowitz, 1977, pp.1095–6), *The Modern World-System* precipitated a minor avalanche of reviews. It will be impossible to consider them in detail. However, it may be noted that even favourable reviewers mentioned the lack of precision in conceptualisation (Hechter, 1975, pp.221, 222) and the lack of clarity in identifying the mechanisms of the capitalist world-economy (p.222; Janowitz, 1977, p.1093). While some economic historians found his model helpful to their own concerns (Thirsk, 1977), others found that it ignored or at least misdescribed the relationship between agrarian class structures and the market (Brenner, 1977). The failure to specify the dynamics of capitalist development (Skocpol, 1977, p.1078) as opposed to the 'forms of appearance of capitalism' (Aronowitz, 1981, p.520), the reliance upon functionalism (p.509) or teleological reasoning (Skocpol, 1977, pp.1078, 1088), the tendency to reductionism (pp.1078–81, 1089), the vagueness with respect to 'the inputed process of causality' and the difficulty of identifying 'that which is to be explained' (Janowitz, 1977, p.1096) were also mentioned.

Skocpol made some telling comments on the need to consider inter-state relations as expressing dynamics which are not reducible to the rhythms of capitalist economic development (1977, pp.1087–8). It is ironic that Moore, whose work is often considered to neglect such factors, provided in one of his earliest articles a preliminary sketch of the dynamics of coalitions and counter-coalitions in the international arena (1955, p.114), a theme he developed further in later work, albeit briefly (1972, pp.33–4, 36–7). The potentiality of such an approach has been explored more recently with reference to the work of both Moore and Wallerstein (Smith, 1978).

The process of evaluating Wallerstein's work remains far from complete, as does the work itself. Perhaps a major difference between his approach and that of Moore is that whereas Wallerstein offers a set of relatively flexible *formulae* (core/periphery, world-system, etc.) which may be applied in a variety of contexts, Moore offers a series of closely related *problems* (What is a rational society? How may misery be reduced or abolished? And so on) which offer difficult questions rather than attractive answers.[11]

Ideology and emancipation

Having considered Moore as a sociologist and historian, attention will now be focused upon Moore as a political theorist. It is impossible to ignore two issues. The first concerns the implications of the work carried out by writers such as Quentin Skinner and J. G. A. Pocock for Moore's objective of making empirical generalisations about the moral codes which have governed relations between rulers and ruled in past and present societies. The second issue concerns the contribution Moore's work may make to the objective invoked by Richard Bernstein of 'restructuring' social and political theory.

Throughout Moore's work there is a tension between a sense that political and other concepts change from one epoch to the next and a conviction that in these successive formulations of 'knowledge' or 'truth' are contained certain unchanging elements which derive from the constants of human nature. The element of contingency is stressed when Moore is insisting upon the need to perceive that the 'inevitable' might be subject to change through human agency. The element of universality is stressed when Moore is insisting that the moral code he is outlining is based not only upon reason but also upon a very wide range of human experience. However, in gathering his 'evidence' in *Injustice* he patently fails to conduct a detailed analysis of the linguistic forms and the range of meanings available to his various witnesses protesting against injustice. Nor does he consider their complaints and proposals in terms of contemporary debates, awareness of whose emphases and silences would help to identify the intended illocutionary force of the various statements which he quotes.

These strictures are not intended to apply to Moore's particular analysis of the German materials but to his larger ambition of identifying universal elements in moral codes. The latter seems incompatible with the spirit of Skinner's contention that a study of classic texts reveals 'not the essential sameness, but rather the essential variety of viable moral assumptions and political commitments' (Skinner, 1969, p.52).[12] A possible defence to the effect that variation in political and moral ideas at the social level occupied by the writers of such texts may coincide with an essential sameness in moral ideas among the lower orders is weakened by Moore's assumption that the moral codes with which he is concerned are appealed to by both rulers and ruled.

Moore marches apparently disregardingly through the mine-fields which writers such as Skinner and Pocock have recently identified for those seeking to understand the political thought of other ages. One more example will be given. In the essay on totalitarianism in pre-industrial societies which I discussed in Chapter 3 Moore examines extracts from the *Book of Lord Shang*, a compilation originating from China in the third century B.C. He finds within it 'several striking parallels with modern totalitarian thought and practice' (1958, p.47). Although he warns that the thought of the Chinese Legalists presented in the *Book of Lord Shang* should be understood 'in its historical context' (p.52), he conducts a comparison of its contents with documents and related evidence from other times and places and concludes that 'Of all the cases examined, the ideas of the Legalists in ancient China display the closest resemblance to modern doctrines of centralized totalitarianism'. He then proceeds to list the similarities, ranging from 'an emphasis on a strong state to the exclusion of other aims and values' to a 'stress on the virtue of an agrarian life' (p.77). The strong implication is that totalitarianism is a coherent and recurrent set of ideas, values and practices which is not contingent upon the conditions of modern industrial society.

One may contrast the approach to the same documents by J. G. A. Pocock in *Politics, Language and Time* (1971, pp.62–6). Pocock argues that although the modern West is 'the home of totalitarian government . . . there is little or nothing in Western totalitarian theory to equal *The Book of Lord Shang*' (p.64). In fact Pocock introduces this text as part of a review of the paradigms discoverable in ancient Chinese philosophy. One of his objects is to stress the *dissimilarities* between Chinese political thought and Western thought:

> we know that Greek and classical Western political thought are distinguished from the Chinese by the possession of a plurality of political forms, a plurality of social and other values, a moral philosophy which asks pressingly how these pluralities came to exist, a profound divergence between physical and political theory, and a way of life which makes the citizen's role in decision-making a principal index of his social position and a formative influence upon his personality. The Greek political

> vocabulary is thus largely our own; whereas if there are Chinese words to be translated as 'liberty', 'citizen', 'autocracy', 'monarch' or for that matter 'politics', it has not become necessary for this investigation to become acquainted with them. (Pocock, 1971, p.78)

However, while the above discussion suggests that in one respect Moore's ambition may have been misguided, there is still an impressive intellectual structure remaining. The final task is to consider the relevance of Moore's work to the project of a writer who insists that 'human beings are capable of bringing to consciousness the interpretations, evaluations, and standards that they tacitly accept, and can subject them to rational criticism' (Bernstein, 1979, p.236). In *The Restructuring of Social and Political Theory*, Richard Bernstein presents a sympathetic but critical analytical review of three orientations which have challenged the understanding that social science is a kind of natural science organised in terms of empirical theory. Among the propositions discussed by Bernstein are that people's beliefs are in fact constitutive of their practices and institutions and that the interpretative models which penetrate thought and action have to be studied if we wish to understand what men and women are. To ignore this requirement and to concentrate exclusively upon observable and measurable behaviour is to neglect the fact that such behaviour expresses values and, by implication, to accept these values uncritically (pp.61-3). A means of avoiding this prospect is offered by the development of normative (as opposed to empirical) theory. Normative theory entails the rational evaluation of the quality of social and political life (p.228).

The first orientation examined by Bernstein draws upon analytical philosophy, especially in its concern with the language of action. This orientation encompasses writers such as Isaiah Berlin, Peter Winch and Thomas Kuhn. While noting that Kuhn's discussion of paradigms has been interpreted in several different ways, he identifies a central issue as being the need to make explicit the concepts and models which produce the biases built into the language used in, for example, the political sphere (pp.110, 111).[13] This first orientation has helped to create a new universe of discourse whose participants are more aware of the ways in which conceptual understandings shape reality (p.113). The second orientation studied, the 'phenomenological alternative', offers a methodology for studying the processes just described. Ideally, the observer should adopt a detached attitude in order to achieve knowledge of the processes whereby meaning is constituted in subjectivity and intersubjectivity.

Unfortunately, the approaches associated with Schutz and Husserl raise further problems. In our studies of 'structures of the life world' how do we distinguish 'those structures which are presumably fixed, permanent and a priori from those which have specific roots and causes'? (p.159) How do we relate an understanding of motives to the procedures of causal analysis? (pp.166–7) How do we evaluate different forms of reality? (p.168) This last issue directs attention to a third orientation, that of critical theory. Reviewing the work of Jürgen Habermas at some length, Bernstein expresses considerable approval for a thinker who moves beyond the notion of the theorist as disinterested observer in order to stress the relationship between knowledge and human interests, especially the interest in moral and political emancipation. I shall return to Bernstein's discussion of Habermas shortly, but first I want to contrast the above highly truncated and selective account of Bernstein's remarkable book with a review of some of the key moments and abiding tensions in Moore's development as a social and political theorist.

As has been noticed, Moore began his work as a comparative sociologist within the framework of empirical theory, a positivist in the mainstream of social science who attempted to correlate variables in order to test hypotheses (Moore, 1942). By the time he had established himself as a Soviet specialist in the early 1950s, Moore was a strong critic of positivism on the grounds that 'Larger problems of the social milieu and, ultimately, of philosophy enter into any defensible judgement of scientific problems' (1958, p.94). He went on to call for the development of a viable normative theory, raising the hope that it might be possible 'to construct a system of values or to find a rational basis for criticising and evaluating society and human behaviour' (p.106). Much of Moore's subsequent work has been concerned with eliciting the rationality expressed in different forms of social order, rationality in terms of the perceived interests of participants in the social order as shaped by their experience of social insecurity and social constraints.

In *Social Origins*, analysis of the motivations or intentions of actors, interpreted with reference to their perceived moral and material interests, was combined with a consideration of changing structural constraints, especially those associated with commercialisation and bureaucratisation, in his presentation of 'causal processes'. As has been seen, an attempt was also made to consider the moral effects of social action through the analysis of what I have labelled 'consequential processes'. An important theme of his later work, *Injustice*, was the attempt to distinguish between some aspects of social relations, including evaluations, which might be shown within the limits of empirical investigation to be present in practically all complex societies and other aspects which are subject to contingency. In other words, in the course of his work from the 1940s onwards Barrington Moore has exemplified the disenchantment with 'mainstream' empirical social science and the search for a way of 'restructuring' social and political theory which Bernstein has described. A number of passages in *Reflections on the Causes of Human Misery* and *Injustice* show the general outlines of the position towards which Moore is moving.

A major premise is that there is no alternative to science conceived as 'valid inference from adequate evidence', a practice whose essence is 'the refusal to believe on the basis of hope' and whose pursuit is not necessarily tied to the search for domination. Indeed, the aesthetic component is very apparent in the higher reaches of science (1972, p.136). Such practices are to be distinguished from the assumption by scientists of the mantle of the priest, a possibility made more likely by popular ignorance about science and the absence of informed criticism: 'In a nutshell, modern man does not know why *not* to believe' (p.56).[14] In fact, the pursuit of rationality through 'full and free discussion of any and all sorts of viewpoints on all subjects' requires: international and internal peace and stability; a rational and educated population with a 'rough equality' in their economic and political capacities; some controls over the rate of innovation in order to preserve social stability; and participants who 'possess both technical and more general intellectual competence' (pp.85–7). The education system would have to equip citizens with the means to grasp 'the basic intellectual issues in the natural and social sciences' (p.87).

In the course of social development critical reflection upon the structural changes which occur has gradually transformed the concepts in terms of which men and women perceive the world, especially notions of inevitability and the role of human agency (1978, pp.489–96). Implicit in the language of human beings is 'a general ground plan, a conception of what social relationships ought to be', a conception which can have 'a critical cutting edge' (p.509). The realisation of such concepts, or at least action guided by the hope of such realisation, depends upon the existence of a major group with the incentive and the power to do something about it.

Moore occasionally refers to the American black population as candidates for this role but never with real conviction (1958, p.183; 1969a, p.154; 1972, p.191). In any case there is a large and irreducible element of risk entailed in practical revolutionary activity. This is due to the impossibility of predicting the future and the likelihood of engendering immoral forms of repression and domination whether the revolution is a failure or a success (1972, pp.38–9, 192). Moore will not allow the would-be revolutionary to justify his or her actions with reference to some notion of 'inevitability' deriving from a critical theory. The revolutionary must take moral responsibility for his or her own actions. Similarly, the responsibility of the intellectual is to pursue rationality and truth for its own sake and 'let the political chips fall where they may' (1972, p.9).

Moore's approach to social analysis persistently draws out the implications for each other of theory and practice, empirical investigation and normative assessment, description and prescription, fact and value. Much of Moore's later work is an attempt to reinstate theory as a rational discussion of moral objectives and to relate this discussion to a reasoned evaluation of possible forms of practice. Like Habermas, he keeps a weather eye open for a class with a practical interest in emancipation. Like Habermas, also he recognises that

> the more the growth and change of society are determined by the more extreme rationality of processes of research, subject to a division of labour, the less rooted is this civilization, now rendered scientific, in the knowledge and conscience of its citizens. (Habermas, 1974, p.256)

Moore also shares Habermas's recognition that the conditions for

the pursuit of knowledge and emancipation ideally include 'a form
of discourse in which there is no other compulsion but the compulsion of argumentation itself', where there is 'genuine symmetry
among the participants involved' and where 'no form of domination exists' (Bernstein, 1979, p.212). Perhaps it is not surprising
that such a convergence has occurred given that Moore has found
intellectual sustenance in debate with men such as Herbert Marcuse and Otto Kirchheimer and has been greatly influenced by the
work of Franz Neumann.[15] Nor is it surprising to find that a recent
attempt to discuss the incorporation of the English working class in
the nineteenth century from the standpoint of critical theory
should refer to three of Moore's works (Hearn, 1978, pp.5, 230,
295–6).

I am certainly not suggesting that Moore is an 'American Habermas', a characterisation which might upset adherents of two great
writers. However, there is a broad overlap of concerns. Moore has
perhaps paid more attention than Habermas to the issues surrounding human agency, a theme which has recurred on several
occasions in this present book. Moore's analysis of the German
working class does seem to have some bearing on the issues raised
in Bernstein's question, directed at Habermas:

> under what conditions will agents who have a clear understand-
> ing of their historical situation be motivated to overcome dis-
> torted communication and strive towards an ideal form of com-
> munity life? What are the concrete dynamics of this process?
> Who are or will become its agents? (Bernstein, 1979, p.224)

If only by showing in some details the obstacles both to 'clear
understanding' and effective action, Moore's analysis carries this
debate forward.

Despite the methodological critique to which a Skinnerian critique may subject it, *Injustice* (especially the historical analysis of
German materials) does seem to be a work which meets a number
of the criteria specified by Bernstein for contributions to the process
of restructuring social and political theory:

> The turning of attention to the analysis of practices, forms of
> life, and subjective meanings, and to understanding how social
> and political life consists of *moral* paradigms, enables us to see

what underlies and is presupposed by the study of regularities and correlations . . . We must . . . ask whether there are systematic distortions or ideological mystifications in the agents' understanding of what they are doing. We must investigate the causes of these distortions and mystifications. We could not even begin to make a distinction between what human beings think they are doing and what they are actually doing, unless we appeal to independent evidence that reveals this disparity. (Bernstein, 1979, p.231)[16]

In the last few pages of his book Bernstein notices and warmly approves of the fact that the function of critique in the work of Habermas is complemented by an argument developed in various philosophical discussions of the language of action. This argument insists that

political and social theory is to be construed as genuine moral theory – 'moral theory' in a sense that is much closer to the understanding of the human sciences as 'moral sciences' in the eighteenth-century sense of this expression. (Bernstein, 1979, p.234)

That, of course, is where we came in.

Notes

Chapter 1

1. *Italics* in original.
2. Initially published by Oxford University Press, New York. The quotations given are from the edition published by Penguin Books in 1970. It should be noted that Moore's collection of essays, *Political Power and Social Theory*, which dealt with similar themes, had appeared in 1958.
3. Barrington Moore's aversion to the over-formalisation of theory and his sensitivity to 'conservative bias' in statistical method both indicate a degree of intellectual kinship with Mills. See Moore (1969a, p.x and appendix). References will be made to the edition of *Social Origins* published by Penguin Books in 1969.
4. *Italics* in original.
5. *Italics* in original.

Chapter 2

1. See Richter (1977), Aron (1965), Bailyn (1967) and Gay (1968).
2. Moore deliberately harks back to the eighteenth century at the beginning of *Reflections on the Causes of Human Misery* (Moore, 1972, p.xi).
3. The debt which the following account owes to Peter Gay's work on the Enlightenment will be obvious. I have followed his practice of naturalising the term 'philosophe' and dropping the italics (Gay, 1967, p.4).
4. On Ferguson see Kettler (1965).
5. On Smith and his predecessors see Letwin (1963). On Bentham see Hutchinson (1956). For the early stages of what promises to be a valuable debate see also Camic (1979), Jones (1981) and Camic (1981).
6. *Italics* in original.
7. The implications of Newton's discoveries in calculus and with respect to gravity for the status of the Deity were debated against Leibniz by Samuel Clarke, spurred on by Voltaire. Newton himself refused to recognise a conflict between science and religion. See, for example, Gay (1969, pp.140–5).
8. The military analogy is significant: 'In science, as in war, we are compelled to make estimates about promising and unpromising lines of attack' (Moore, 1958, p.112).
9. Moore wrote in the 1950s that American society 'at the present conjuncture a prosperous country at a high point in its power . . . has some of the qualities of an *ancien régime*' (Moore, 1958, p.139).

10. This paper originally appeared in *World Politics*, (1), 6, October 1953, pp.122–38. It was reprinted in *Political Power and Social Theory* and references are made to this location.
11. Moore's comments in *Social Origins* on the logical difficulties of trying to use sampling techniques to analyse historical change are anticipated in Moore (1958, pp.131–6).

Chapter 3

1. Wolff *et al.* (1969), Moore and Wolff (1967).
2. See Marcuse (1941).
3. See, for example, Moore (1947, pp.734–5).
4. 'Tolerance and the scientific outlook' originally appeared in the USA in 1967 but the references are to the British edition of 1969.
5. Bentham (1965, ch. 2), Gay (1969, pp.459–61).
6. Gresham's law, originally formulated with respect to currency, asserts that the 'bad' will drive out the 'good'. Cf. Moore (1955, p.114).
7. Compare the following comment by Adam Ferguson: 'Without the rivalship of nations, and the practice of war, civil society itself could scarcely have found a form' (1980, p.24).

Chapter 4

1. On the cyclical tendencies in Bolshevik ideological debate see Moore (1950, p.39).
2. Cf. Moore (1954, pp.196–7).
3. 'Where the expression "we" does occur, it refers to the reader as a companion in the search for truth' (Moore, 1958, p.ix).
4. Just to cite the first three chapters: the English case contains a series of specific comparisons with Russia (pp.7,11,16,30), China (pp.7,16,30), Germany (pp.30,32,34,35,36,37,38), Japan (p.30) and Spain (p.7); the French study cites Russia (pp.57,70–1), China (pp.53,57), Germany (pp.43,108,109), Japan (pp.53,57,109), India (pp.57,101) alongside twenty-two cross-references to England; the American case study directs attention to Russia (pp.110,153), China (p.110), France (pp.110,121,141,153), Germany (pp.115,141,152), England (pp.110,114,121,140,141,153), Greece (p.123) and Rome (pp.123,154). So it continues throughout the book, each cross-reference a careful stitch in the fabric.
5. Moore refers to Adam Smith's work quite frequently (e.g. 1950, p.298; 1955, p.107; 1969a, p.8; 1978, pp.85,128,135).
6. Moore's wartime career should not be regarded as decisive. As has been seen, Herbert Marcuse was employed in a broadly similar way during the war and continued to develop an approach whose assumptions about Russia and America are in many ways different from those expressed by Moore.

7. In a subsequent article Moore acknowledges that 'World War II and subsequent allied occupation constituted an *ersatz* revolution' in Germany and Japan (1968, p.4). He also acknowledges implicitly that the outcome of the Napoleonic wars had an important impact on the development of democracy in England (1969a, p.31). However, the importance of war for the development of democracy in France is a neglected theme in his work.

8. Moore describes one example of a national intelligentsia and the constraints under which it operates in *Terror and Progress USSR* (1954, pp.114–53). See also Moore (1972, pp.91–104).

9. For a valuable review see Johnson (1976, esp. pp.15–18).

10. To cite just one example, E. P. Thompson's *The Making of the English Working Class* had appeared in 1963. For my own approach see Smith (1982). On Thompson's work, see Chapter 6.

11. *Italics* in original.

Chapter 5

1. Other books on a similar theme appearing at this time included Fainsod (1953) and Rostow (1953).

2. Ciliga (1940, p.102).

3. Reviews of *Injustice* include Wiener (1979), Sheehan (1980), Tenfelde (1980) and Rubenstein (1980).

4. The following comments are based upon Smith (1982, esp. chs 2,3,4 and 7).

5. The importance of this question had been signalled in his earliest work. In *Soviet Politics* Moore indicates not only the considerable importance of foreign relations for understanding the development of the Soviet state but also the particular significance of the failure of the attempted German revolution just after the end of the First World War. The Russian leaders had been relying upon 'the logic of history' to provide them with a powerful and friendly workers' state to the West which would shield them from the 'forces of imperialism' (1950, pp.196–7). Twenty-eight years later Moore comments: 'it is fair to ask what might have happened in the world at large had a socialist revolution occurred in Germany soon after defeat. Would socialism in *both* Germany and Russia have eased the strain on socialist modernization in such a way as to avert the horrors of Stalinism? Would the Allies have been willing and able to stop its triumphant march?' (1978, p.397: *italics* in original).

6. *Italics* in original.

7. This 'other book' might be well described as 'a moral argument with historical illustrations', to quote the subtitle of Michael Walzer's *Just and Unjust Wars*, which appeared in 1977. For a critique of Walzer's book see Hoffman (1981).

8. Cf. Moore (1942).

9. The interplay of these themes in American intellectual life with the

Spencerian tendencies of, for example, Sumner and Keller, would merit further investigation. Moore owed his 'original training in the social sciences' and his interest in Russian affairs to Albert Keller of Yale (Moore, 1950, p.xiii). On Sumner and Keller see Harris (1968, pp.608–11). On original sin and the Garden of Eden see Hollis (1981) and Kurtz (1979). I am grateful for helpful discussion on these points to Val Riddell of the American Studies Department of the University of Leicester.

Chapter 6

1. *Italics* in original.
2. References to the 'Open letter to Leslek Kolakowski' and 'The peculiarities of the English' will be taken from Thompson (1978), where they are reprinted.
3. Perhaps it is possible to discern a slight difference in emphasis between their approaches to 'law and order'. Thompson has tended to stress the value of the rule of law as providing an arena within which conflicts can be fought out with some hope of justice (1975, pp.264–6), whereas Moore tends to manifest a Hobbesian awareness that the penalties of disorder are at least as great as those of order without justice (1972, p.62).
4. Describing the handloom weavers' plight in the early nineteenth century, Thompson writes that the elimination of 'painful and obsolete work' might be justified. 'But this is an argument which discounts the suffering of one generation against the gains of the future. For those who suffered, this retrospective comfort is cold' (1968, p.346). Moore's work is, of course, full of similar sentiments. Another similarity in methodology, which cannot be explored here, is the use by both Thompson and Moore of the 'history-game in which we suppose that A did not happen and B (which did not happen) did' (Thompson, 1978, p.46) and also their exploration of possible futures in terms of a similar logic (pp.71–2).
5. *Italics* in original.
6. *Italics* in original.
7. *Italics* in original.
8. The article cited derives similar conclusions to those of Skocpol about certain aspects of social revolution in France, China and Russia (Smith, 1978, pp.194–7, 199–202, 205–7).
9. *Italics* in original.
10. This article is reprinted in Etzioni and Dubow (1970) in an abbreviated form. This collection also contains extracts from J. S. Mill's *A System of Logic*, where he sets out the 'method of agreement' and the 'method of difference'.
11. Explicit use has been made of Moore's formulations in *Social Origins* by, for example, Dore and Óuchi (1971), Castles (1973), Tilton (1974) and Wiener (1975).

12. Moore would presumably agree with Skinner that 'our own society places unrecognized constraints upon our imaginations' and that from the past we learn 'the distinction between what is necessary and what is the product merely of our own contingent arrangements' (Skinner, 1969, p.53). Skinner is indeed prepared to go a little further than this and recognise that 'there may be apparently perennial *questions*, if these are sufficiently abstractly framed' (p.52: *italics* in original). However, there is considerable doubt as to whether the approach to the analysis of political ideas developed in the paper from which these extracts are taken would produce the kind of survey through time and space conducted by Moore in *Injustice*. Nevertheless, both Moore and Skinner have been concerned to mount 'a dialogue between philosophical discussion and historical evidence', and Moore's writings on Russia manifest a concern with 'the conditions under which languages change' (Skinner, 1969, pp.49–50). Moore's sensitivity to the rigidities and preconceptions built into language and to the constraints and potentialities of cultural symbols has already been noticed in the discussion of *Soviet Politics*. Some subtle interrelationships between ways of thinking and political structures were explored at some length by Moore in *Terror and Progress USSR*. Moore, furthermore, devotes some considerable attention to an exploration of the social conditions under which 'moral innovators' such as Martin Luther may arise (Moore, 1978, p.91). Arguing from different premises Skinner investigates, as part of his analysis in *The Foundations of Modern Political Thought*, the ways in which men such as Thomas More and Niccolo Machiavelli were able to make radical innovations in political theory (Skinner, 1978a, pp.128–38, 255–62). For critiques of Skinner's work see, for example, Wiener (1974), Schochet (1974), Mulligan *et al.* (1979), Black (1980) and Boucher (1980).

13. For example, Skinner (1973). Bernstein argues that Pocock's understanding of paradigm is different from that of, among others, Kuhn. See Kuhn (1970), Pocock (1971), Bernstein (1979, p.246).

14. *Italics* in original.

15. Kirchheimer is referred to in Moore (1969b, p.91). See also Kirchheimer (1969).

16. *Italics* in original.

Bibliography

Abrams, P. (1980) 'History, sociology, historical sociology', *Past and Present*, 87, 3–16.

Almond, G. (1967) Review of *Social Origins*, *American Political Science Review*, 61(3) 768–70.

Anderson, M. (1971) *Family Structure in Nineteenth-Century Lancashire*, Cambridge University Press.

Anderson, P. (1974a) *Passages from Antiquity to Feudalism*, London, New Left Books.

Anderson, P. (1974b) *Lineages of the Absolutist State*, London, New Left Books.

Anderson, P. (1980) *Arguments within English Marxism*, London, New Left Books.

Aron, R. (1965) *Main Currents in Sociological Thought. Vol I: Montesquieu, Marx, Tocqueville*, Harmondsworth, Penguin.

Aronowitz, S. (1981) 'A metatheoretical critique of Immanuel Wallerstein's *The Modern World System*', *Theory and Society*, 10, 469–502.

Bailyn, B. (1967) *The Intellectual Origins of the American Revolution*, Cambridge, Mass., Belknap Press.

Barker, E. (ed.) (1960) *Social Contract: Essays by Locke, Hume and Rousseau*, with an introduction by Sir Ernest Barker, London, Oxford University Press.

Baran, P. A. and Sweezy, P. M. (1966) *Monopoly Capital*, New York, Monthly Review Press.

Bendix, R. (1967) Review of *Social Origins*, *Political Science Quarterly*, 32(4) 625–7.

Benson, Lee (1972) *Towards the Scientific Study of History*, Philadelphia, J. B. Lippincott.

Bentham, J. (1965) *The Principles of Morals and Legislation*, with an introduction by L. J. Lafleur, New York, Hafner.

Bernstein, R. J. (1979) *The Restructuring of Social and Political Theory*, London, Methuen.

Black, A. (1980) 'Skinner on "The Foundations of Modern Political Thought"', *Political Studies*, 28(3) 451–7.

Bottomore, T. and Nisbet, R. (eds.) (1979) *A History of Sociological Analysis*, London, Heinemann.

Boucher, D. E. (1980) 'On Shklar's and Franklin's review of Skinner's *The Foundations of Modern Political Thought*', *Political Theory*, 8(3) 406–8.

Brenner, R. (1976) 'Agrarian class structures and economic development in pre-industrial Europe', *Past and Present*, 70, 30–75.

Brenner, R. (1977) 'The origins of capitalist development: a critique of neo-Smithian Marxism', *New Left Review*, 105, 25–92.

Brunton, D. and Pennington, D. H. (1954) *Members of the Long Parliament*, London, Allen & Unwin.

Bryson, G. (1968) *Man and Society: the Scottish Inquiry of the Eighteenth Century*, New York, Kelley.

Burin, F. S. and Shell, K. L. (eds.) (1969) *Politics, Law and Social Change. Selected Essays of Otto Kirchheimer*, New York, Columbia University Press.

Camic, C. (1979) 'The Utilitarians revisited', *American Journal of Sociology*, 85(3) 516–50.

Camic, C. (1981) 'On the methodology of the history of sociology: a reply to Jones', *American Journal of Sociology*, 86(5) 1139–44.

Castles, F. G. (1973) 'Barrington Moore's thesis and Swedish political development', *Government and Opposition*, 8 (3) 313–31.

Ciliga, A. (1940) *The Russian Enigma*, London, The Labour Book Service.

Cohen, M. (1953) *Reason and Nature*, Glencoe, Free Press.

Dawe, A. (1970) 'The two sociologies', *British Journal of Sociology*, 21(2) 207–18.

Dawe, A. (1979) 'Theories of social action', in Bottomore and Nisbet (1979, 362–417).

De Grazia, S. (1948) *The Political Community: A Study in Anomie*, University of Chicago Press.

De Grazia, S. (1952) *Errors of Psychotherapy*, New York, Doubleday.

Dickens, C. (1843) 'A Christmas Carol', in *Christmas Books*, London, Chapman & Hall.

Dore, R. P. (1969) 'Making sense of history', *European Journal of Sociology*, 10(2) 295–305.

Dore, R. P. and Ouchi, T. (1971) 'Rural origins of Japanese fascism', in Morley (1971, 181–209).

Etzioni, A. and Dubow, F. L. (eds.) (1970) *Comparative Perspectives: Theories and Methods*, Boston, Little, Brown.

Fainsod, M. (1953) *How Russia is Ruled*, Cambridge, Mass., Harvard University Press.

Ferguson, A. (1980) *An Essay on the History of Civil Society*, with a new introduction by Louis Schneider (originally published in 1767), London, Transaction Books.

Gay, P. (1967) *The Enlightenment: An Interpretation. Volume One: The Rise of Modern Paganism*, New York, Alfred Knopf.

Gay, P. (1968) 'The Enlightenment', in Woodward (1968, pp.34–46).

Gay, P. (1969) *The Enlightenment: An Interpretation. Volume Two: The Science of Freedom*, New York, Alfred Knopf.

Giddens, A. (1973) *The Class Structure of the Advanced Societies*, London, Hutchinson.

Greer, D. (1935) *The Incidence of the Terror during the French Revolution*, Cambridge, Mass., Harvard University Press.

Gusfield, J. (1967) Review of *Social Origins*, *Social Forces*, 46 (1) 114–15.

Habermas, J. (1974) *Theory and Practice*, London, Heinemann.

Hamburger, J. (1963) *James Mill and the Art of Revolution*, New Haven, Conn., Yale University Press.

Harootunian, H. D. (1968) Review of *Social Origins, Journal of Asian Studies*, 27(2) 372–4.

Harris, M. (1968) *The Rise of Anthropological Theory*, London Routledge & Kegan Paul.

Hearn, F. (1978) *Domination, Legitimation and Resistance: The Incorporation of the Nineteenth-Century English Working Class*, Westwood, Conn.: Greenwood Press.

Hechter, M. (1975) Review of *The Modern World-System, Contemporary Sociology*, 4(3) 217–22.

Himmelstein, J. L. and Kimmel, M. S. (1981) 'States and revolutions: the implications and limits of Skocpol's structural model', *American Journal of Sociology*, 86(5) 1145–54.

Hobsbawm, E. J. (1967) Review of *Social Origins, American Sociological Review*, 32(5) 821–2.

Hobsbawm, E. J. (1980) 'The revival of narrative: some comments', *Past and Present*, 86, 3–8.

Hoffman, S. (1981) 'States and the morality of war', *Political Theory*, 9(2) 149–72.

Hollis, M. (1981) 'Economic man and original sin', *Political Studies*, 29(2) 167–80.

Hopkins, T. K. and Wallerstein, I. (1967) 'The comparative study of national societies', *Social Science Information*, 6(5) 25–58.

Hume, D. (1960) *Of the Original Contract* (originally published 1748), in Barker (1960).

Hume, D. (1961) *A Treatise of Human Nature: Vol. One*, London, Dent (originally published 1737).

Hutchinson, T. W. (1956) 'Bentham as an economist', *Economic Journal*, 66(2) 288–300.

Janowitz, M. (1977) 'A sociological perspective on Wallerstein', *American Journal of Sociology*, 82(5) 1090–6.

Johnson, R. (1976) 'Barrington Moore, Perry Anderson and English social development', *Working Papers in Cultural Studies*, 9, Centre for Contemporary Cultural Studies, Birmingham University.

Jones, J. A. (1981) 'On Camic's antipresentist methodology', *American Journal of Sociology*, 86(5) 1133–8.

Kerner, O. (1968) *Report of National Advisory Commission on Civil Disorders*, with an introduction by Tom Wicker, New York, Bantam.

Kettler, D. (1965) *The Social and Political Thought of Adam Ferguson*, Ohio State University Press.

Kirchheimer, O. (1969) 'Confining conditions and revolutionary breakthroughs', in Burin and Shell (1969, 385–407).

Kolko, G. (1969) *The Roots of American Foreign Policy*, Boston, Beacon Press.

Kroebner, A. L. (1944) *Configurations of Culture Growth*, Berkeley, California University Press.

Kuhn, T. (1970) *The Structure of Scientific Revolutions*, 2nd ed., University of Chicago Press.

Kumar, K. (1976) 'Revolution and industrial society: an historical perspective', *Sociology*, 10(2) 245–69.

Kurtz, L. R. (1979) 'Freedom and domination: the Garden of Eden and the social order', *Social Forces*, 58(2) 443–65.

Lane, C. (1981) *Rites of the Rulers*, Cambridge University Press.

Lane, D. (1976) *The Socialist Industrial State: Towards a Political Sociology of State Socialism*, London, Allen & Unwin.

Lane, D. (1978) *Politics and Society in the USSR*, rev. ed, Oxford, Martin Robertson.

Lenski, G. (1966) *Power and Privilege*, New York, McGraw-Hill.

Letwin, W. (1963) *The Origins of Scientific Economics: English Economic Thought 1660–1776*, London, Methuen.

Levy, M. J. (1952) *The Structure of Society*, Princeton University Press.

Lowenthal, D. (1968) Review of *Social Origins*, *History and Theory*, 7(2) 257–78.

Macfarlane, J. (1976) 'The Denaby Main lock-out of 1885', in Pollard and Holmes (1976, 74–88).

MacIntyre, A. (1970) *Marcuse*, London, Fontana.

Magdoff, H. (1969) *The Age of Imperialism*, New York, Monthly Review Press.

Marcuse, H. (1941) *Reason and Revolution*, New York, Humanities Press.

Marcuse, H. (1958) *Soviet Marxism*, London, Routledge & Kegan Paul.

Marcuse, H. (1964) *One-Dimensional Man*, London, Routledge & Kegan Paul.

Marcuse, H. (1969) *Eros and Civilization*, London, Sphere Books.

Miliband, R. and Saville, J. (eds.) (1965) *The Socialist Register*, London, Merlin Press.

Miliband, R. and Saville, J. (eds.) (1973) *The Socialist Register*, London, Merlin Press.

Mill, J. S. (1888) *A System of Logic*, New York, Harper & Row (originally published 1843).

Mills, C. W. (1970) *The Sociological Imagination*, Harmondsworth, Penguin.

Mingay, G. E. (1962) 'The size of farms in the eighteenth century', *Economic History Review*, 14(3) 469–88.

Moore, B. (1942) 'The relation between social stratification and social control', *Sociometry*, 5(3) 230–50.

Moore, B. (1945) 'A comparative analysis of the class struggle', *American Sociological Review*, 10(1) 31–7.

Moore, B. (1947) 'The influence of ideas on policies as shown in the collectivization of agriculture in Russia', *American Political Science Review*, 41(3) 733–43.

Moore, B. (1950) *Soviet Politics – The Dilemma of Power: The Role of Ideas in Social Change*, Cambridge, Mass.: Harvard University Press.

Moore, B. (1954) *Terror and Progress USSR: Some Sources of Change and Stability in the Soviet Dictatorship*, Cambridge, Mass.: Harvard University Press.

Moore, B. (1955) 'Sociological theory and contemporary politics', *Ameri-*

can Journal of Sociology, 61(2) 107–15.

Moore, B. (1958) *Political Power and Social Theory*, Cambridge, Mass.: Harvard University Press.

Moore, B. (1967) 'The society nobody wants: a look beyond Marxism and Liberalism', in Moore and Wolff (1967, 401–18).

Moore, B. (1968) 'Thoughts on violence and democracy', *Proceedings of the Academy of Political Science*, 29(1) 1–12.

Moore, B. (1969a) *Social Origins of Dictatorship and Democracy: Lord and Peasant in the Making of the Modern World*, Harmondsworth, Penguin.

Moore, B. (1969b) 'Tolerance and the scientific outlook', in Wolff *et al.* (1969, 65–91).

Moore, B. (1972) *Reflections on the Causes of Human Misery and on Certain Proposals to Eliminate Them*, Harmondsworth, Penguin.

Moore, B. (1978) *Injustice: The Social Bases of Obedience and Revolt*, London, Macmillan Press.

Moore, B. and Wolff, K. H. (eds.) (1967) *The Critical Spirit: Essays in Honour of Herbert Marcuse*, Boston, Beacon Press.

Morley, J. W. (ed.) (1971) *Dilemmas of Growth in Pre-War Japan*, Princeton University Press.

Mousnier, R. (1971) *Peasant Uprisings*, London, Allen & Unwin.

Mulligan, L. *et al.* (1979) 'Intentions and conventions: a critique of Quentin Skinner's method for the study of ideas', *Political Studies*, 27(1) 84–98.

Ness, G. D. (1967) Review of *Social Origins*, *American Sociological Review*, 32(4) 818–20.

Nettl, P. (1967) 'Return of the intellectual', *New Statesman*, 6 October.

Neumann, F. L. (1950) 'Approaches to the study of political power', *Political Science Quarterly*, 65(2) 161–80.

Neumann, F. L. (1957) *The Democratic and the Authoritarian State*, Glencoe, Free Press.

Nossiter, R. J. (ed.) (1972) *Imagination and Precision in the Social Sciences*, London, Faber.

Parsons, T. (1951) *The Social System*, London, Routledge & Kegan Paul.

Pocock, J. G. A. (1971) *Politics, Language and Time: Essays on Political Thought and History*, London, Methuen.

Poggi, G. (1968) Review of *Social Origins*, *British Journal of Sociology*, 19(2) 215–17.

Poggi, G. (1978) *The Development of the Modern State: A Sociological Introduction*, London, Hutchinson.

Pollard, S. (1959) *A History of Labour in Sheffield*, Liverpool University Press.

Pollard, S. and Holmes, C. (eds.) (1976) *Essays in the Economic and Social History of South Yorkshire*, Barnsley, South Yorkshire County Council Recreation, Culture and Health Department.

Rawls, J. (1971) *A Theory of Justice*, Oxford University Press.

Richter, M. (1977) *The Political Theory of Montesquieu*, Cambridge University Press.

Rokkan, S. (1972) 'Models and methods in the comparative study of nation-building', in Nossiter (1972, 121–56).
Rosenthal, S. J. (1967) Review of *Social Origins, Monthly Review*, 18(4) 30–6.
Rostow, W. W. (1953) *The Dynamics of Soviet Society*, New York, Norton.
Rothman, S. (1970) 'Barrington Moore and the dialectics of revolution: an essay review', *American Political Science Review*, 64(1) 61–83.
Rubenstein, R. L. (1980) 'Moral outrage as false consciousness', *Theory and Society*, 9, 745–55.
Runciman, W. G. (1980) 'Comparative sociology or narrative history? A note on the methodology of Perry Anderson', *European Journal of Sociology*, 21(1) 162–78.
Salamon, L. M. (1970) 'Comparative history and the theory of modernization', *World Politics*, 23(1) 83–103.
Santayana, G. (1948) *The Life of Reason: Reason in Science*, New York, Scribner.
Schlesinger, A. (1965) *A Thousand Days*, New York, Deutsch.
Schochet, G. J. (1974) 'Quentin Skinner's method', *Political Theory*, 2(3) 261–76.
Shanin, T. (1971) *Peasants and Peasant Societies*, Harmondsworth, Penguin.
Shapiro, G. (1967) Review of *Social Origins, American Sociological Review*, 32(5) 820–1.
Sheehan, J. J. (1980) 'Barrington Moore on obedience and revolt', *Theory and Society*, 9(5) 723–34.
Skinner, Q. (1969) 'Meaning and understanding in the history of ideas', *History and Theory*, 8(1) 3–53.
Skinner, Q. (1973) 'The empirical theorists of democracy and their critics: a plague on both their houses', *Political Theory*, 1(3) 287–306.
Skinner, Q. (1978a) *The Foundations of Modern Political Thought. Volume One: The Renaissance*, Cambridge University Press.
Skinner, Q. (1978b) *The Foundations of Modern Political Thought: Volume Two: The Reformation*, Cambridge University Press.
Skocpol, T. (1973) 'A critical review of Barrington Moore's *Social Origins of Dictatorship and Democracy*', *Politics and Society*, 4(1) 1–34.
Skocpol, T. (1977) 'Wallerstein's world-capitalist system: a theoretical and historical critique', *American Journal of Sociology*, 82(5) 1075–90.
Skocpol, T. (1979) *States and Social Revolutions: A Comparative Analysis of France, Russia and China*, Cambridge University Press.
Smith, A. (1976) *An Inquiry into the Nature and Causes of the Wealth of Nations* (originally published in 1776), ed. R. H. Campbell *et al.*, 2 vols, Oxford, Clarendon Press.
Smith, D. (1978) 'Domination and containment: an approach to modernization', *Comparative Studies in Society and History*, 20(2) 177–213.
Smith, D. (1982) *Conflict and Compromise: Class Formation in English Society 1830–1914. A Comparative Study of Birmingham and Sheffield*, London, Routledge & Kegan Paul.

Somers, R. H. (1971) 'Application of an expanded survey research model to comparative studies', in Vallier (1971, 357–420).

Stinchcombe, A. L. (1967) Review of *Social Origins, Harvard Educational Review*, 37(2) 290–3.

Stone, L. (1979) 'The revival of narrative: reflections on a new old history', *Past and Present*, 85, 3–24.

Sumner, W. G. (1960) *Folkways*, New York, Mentor (originally published 1906).

Tenfelde, K. (1980) 'German workers and the incapacity for revolution', *Theory and Society*, 9(5) 735–44.

Thirsk, J. (1977) 'Economic and social development on a European-world scale', *American Journal of Sociology*, 82(5) 1097–1102.

Thompson, E. P. (1963) *The Making of the English Working Class*, Harmondsworth, Penguin.

Thompson, E. P. (1965) 'The peculiarities of the English', in Miliband and Saville (1965, 311–62).

Thompson, E. P. (1971) 'The moral economy of the English crowd in the eighteenth century', *Past and Present*, 50, 76–136.

Thompson, E. P. (1973) 'An open letter to Leslek Kolakowski', in Miliband and Saville (1973, 1–100).

Thompson, E. P. (1975) *Whigs and Hunters*, London, Allen Lane.

Thompson, E. P. (1978) *The Poverty of Theory*, London, Merlin Press.

Tilton, T. A. (1974) 'The social origins of liberal democracy: the Swedish case', *American Political Science Review*, 68(2) 561–71.

Tolstoy, L. N. (1954) *Anna Karenina* trans. R. Edmonds, Harmondsworth, Penguin.

Vallier, I. (ed.) (1971) *Comparative Methods in Sociology: Essays on Trends and Applications*, Berkeley, University of California Press.

Wallerstein, I. (1974) *The Modern World-System: Capitalist Agriculture and the Origins of the European World-Economy in the Sixteenth Century*, New York, Academic Press.

Wallerstein, I. (1980a) *The Capitalist World-Economy*, Cambridge University Press.

Wallerstein, I. (1980b) *The Modern World-System II. Mercantilism and the Consolidation of the European World-Economy 1600–1750*, New York, Academic Press.

Walzer, M. (1977) *Just and Unjust Wars: A Moral Argument with Historical Illustrations*, Harmondsworth, Penguin.

Wiener, J. M. (1974) 'Quentin Skinner's Hobbes', *Political Theory*, 2(3) 251–60.

Wiener, J. M. (1975) 'Planter–merchant conflict in Reconstruction Alabama', *Past and Present*, 68, 73–94.

Wiener, J. M. (1976) 'Review of reviews', *History and Theory*, 15(2) 146–75.

Wiener, J. M. (1979) 'Working-class consciousness in Germany, 1848–1933', *Marxist Perspectives*, 5(2) 156–69.

Whitehead, A. N. (1938) *Modes of Thought*, Cambridge University Press.

Williams, R. (1963) *Culture and Society*, Harmondsworth, Penguin.

Wolf, E. R. (1971) *Peasant Wars of the Twentieth Century*, London, Faber.

Wolff, R. P. *et al.* (1969) *A Critique of Pure Tolerance*, London, Jonathan Cape.

Woodward, C. Vann (ed.) (1968) *The Comparative Approach to American History*, New York, Basic Books.

Zagorin, P. (1973) 'Theories of revolution in contemporary historiography', *Political Science Quarterly*, 88(1) 23–52.

Zukin, S. (1980) 'Introduction to Barrington Moore symposium', *Theory and Society*, 9, 721–2.

Index